THE GOVERNANCE

OF COMMON PROPERTY

RESOURCES

The governance

of common property

PAPERS PRESENTED resources

AT A FORUM CONDUCTED BY RESOURCES

FOR THE FUTURE, INC. IN WASHINGTON, D.C.

JANUARY 21–22, 1974   Edited by

Edwin T. Haefele

Published for Resources for the Future, Inc.
by The Johns Hopkins University Press,
Baltimore and London

Copyright © 1974 by Resources for the Future, Inc.
All rights reserved
Manufactured in the United States of America
Library of Congress Catalog Card Number 74-6825
ISBN 0-8018-1650-5

Library of Congress Cataloging in Publication data will be found on the last printed page of this book.

Contents

THE GOVERNANCE

OF COMMON PROPERTY

RESOURCES

EDWIN T. HAEFELE

Introduction

OWNERSHIP, within some limits, implies control. If I own my house, I can sell it, tear it down, rent to someone else or, perhaps, paint it. If I am rational, I will normally do nothing that will decrease its value but will, on the other hand, be inclined to do things that will enhance its value. Not all of the physical universe is "owned" in this sense, and of the things that are owned, not all are owned by private parties who are presumed to be economic maximizers.

Among the unowned things are the oceans, the air mantle, and most of the rivers and lakes of the world. Non–privately owned things include the public lands of the United States, parks, public buildings, and the lands under the rivers (most of which are owned by the bordering states).

Common property resources refer both to those things no one owns and to those things that all of us own. In both cases someone has to decide who may control the resource, who may use it, and under what circumstances. It might be thought that no such system of control need be considered, but at least in the Old World it has been a settled fact since Aristotle that common property resources, like private property resources, needed governance. In the New World such wisdom has been long in coming and is still bitterly resented in some quarters. We are the children of those who settled the last "empty" continent, a continent of endless land and air and water. We now grudgingly acknowledge that all are finite and take up the chore of making decisions about air and water pollution with an ill-concealed sense of being somehow put-upon.

We find, moreover, that decision making on common property resources may take place through a variety of collective choice mech-

The author is Director, Regional and Urban Studies Program, Resources for the Future, Inc.

1

anisms. That is, decisions may be made through the courts, by legislative action, in executive agency or appointed commission, or by referendum vote. The decision arrived at by one mechanism will not, except by chance, be the same as would be arrived at by another mechanism. Those who feel their interests are better served by one than by another become advocates. Thus, some California voters, sensing their lack of success in influencing the legislature, turned to referendum to pass a land use control measure for the California coast. The measure itself sets up a commission insulated from direct voter pressure. Who will be able to influence the commission?

The growth of the environmental law movement in the late 1960s was a response to a growing sense of frustration over executive agency actions (or lack thereof) and legislative enactments of unparalleled vagueness. Few would argue, however, that an adversary proceeding necessarily brings out third-party effects, that is, effects not relevant to the dispute at issue. Such third-party effects may be at the heart of a distributional resolution of the problem (which a legislature could speak to) or may be intimately bound up in the efficient solution that accounts for externalities (which economic analysis can speak to).

One may contend, without greatly distorting the facts, that neither executive governance, legislative governance, nor judicial governance has proven adequate (singly or in combination) to deal with common property resources. That may be why we have tended, in recent years, toward the creation of the quasi-judicial, quasi-legislative, quasi-executive (and quasi-effective) commissions and boards that always appear when normal governance mechanisms fail us. While these devices have little to recommend them, they do have one overwhelming virtue; they get out of the way for awhile the problem that is loading ordinary governments beyond capacity. Beginning with the creation of the Interstate Commerce Commission in the late 1800s (at a time when railroad rate questions threatened to overwhelm regular government machinery), we have always been able to buy time by establishing a new form of decision making.

In common property resource management, we may be at that point, with the courts clogged with environmental cases and the legislatures and executive agencies seemingly incapable of coming to decisions that do not alienate more than they placate. Certainly if we judge by public statements, both those dedicated to conservation and those dedicated to development seem about equally convinced that their causes are in imminent danger.

2

Perhaps it would be useful to pose some of the questions on which decisions must be made: How clean should the air be? How much of the federally owned land should be preserved in wilderness? How much development should be allowed along the seacoast? Should all reaches of all rivers be made suitable for swimming? If not, which rivers are to be favored? Should there be national standards for allowable pollution? Regional standards? Local standards? Should communities be allowed to zone out some activities and types of housing? What development should be allowed along river banks?

Back of all these queries, and others, are the governance questions: Who should decide? What process should be used in coming to the decision? The papers assembled in this volume stem from an RFF forum on common property resources. The authors and other participants in the forum were asked to focus on the governance questions from the vantage point of their respective disciplines. While the analyses presented are by no means definitive, we are given the best answers at present available from economics and the law—the two disciplines most heavily represented. It will be instructive to examine how each discipline poses the problem.

The economists are, in general, concerned with the construction of an appropriate theory and methodology that will lead us to a "correct" answer to the substantive problems of use of common property resources. In other words, one should choose a process because of the answers it produces. If it produces the correct answer, it is the right process and, by inference, anyone who will use this right process that comes to the correct answer is the appropriate person to make the decision. This is slightly overdrawn, but only slightly. The economists admit difficulties relating to the practicality of compensation of losers by winners in a Pareto-optimal solution, and they recognize the problem of unequal resources (money) among the competitors for the use of common property. Moreover, they see that the producer has an organization and motivation vastly superior to those of myriad consumers, so that in any contest for influence over events in whatever arena the producer is apt to win. This remains true in spite of some highly publicized wins in recent years by consumer advocates.

It is perhaps only the historian and lawyer who can see that putting one's faith in a process that comes to correct decisions is a dangerous business. The same process may turn into a club that can be used effectively by one's worst enemies. The lawyer, in particular, will look more to the process itself than to the results obtained by using it in the instant

3

case. Legal procedures are one of man's early attempts to build a *general* problem-solving algorithm long before the advent of the computer. (As Professor Rosenblum points out in his paper, the results are something short of predictable.) The legal process remains, however, a process that attempts to be "correct," never mind the results that obtain from using it.

There is yet another point of view represented in the papers, the point of view of social (collective) choice theory. This theory, developed on the boundary between economics and political science, suffers from the common fate of border dwellers—it is constantly overrun by one side or the other. It gives equal attention to process and to outcomes, and focuses typically on an examination of alternative structures or mechanisms of choice. The theory is in a rudimentary stage, but it does allow us to think, I hope constructively, about the governance problem in much the same way our ancestors would have two centuries or more ago. The widespread and persistent third-party effects of all our decisions, public and private, could not have been anticipated when our basic governmental forms and processes were put in place. The extent to which business firms, i.e., the multinational corporations controlling fortunes larger than many countries and most of our states, would dominate our political processes was not contemplated in 1787. Both developments have put severe burdens on our governmental structure at all levels and in all branches. Whether or not we can continue, in any real sense, to be a country governed by the consent of the governed, is by no means clear. (Those of us who write and read books may be the last to know.) How we deal with our common property resources may well provide a clue to our abilities to cope with the generic problem of self-government.

Many of these papers have arguments presented in mathematical form. I hope the use of these symbols, a convenient shorthand to the initiated, will not deter others from following the arguments. Persistence is a virtue, and there are few pages in what follows that cannot be understood, in essence, by the determined humanist.

ROBERT DORFMAN

The technical basis for
decision making

MY TASK is a very important and difficult one. It is no less than to set forth a fruitful conceptual framework for the discussions to follow. It is also a very great privilege, because it gives me the opportunity, before anyone else can present their view, to advocate my own penchants and to derogate other people's, which I fully intend to do.

First of all, I have to address myself to the concept of common property resources. Each of us knows what they are, generally speaking, but as I read the literature I am sure that we are not all in exact agreement. By that I mean that there are many questionable cases in which I should say, "This is a common property resource," and you would say, "It is not." As a homely example, consider ski slopes. Some are privately owned but nevertheless can, and do, give rise to serious congestion problems on occasion. They are not common property resources as commonly understood. But the slope on the next mountain may be in a public park. Is that a common property resource, or is it also a private resource that happens to be owned by the state? I am not going to insist on an answer, since we could waste a great deal of time if we attempted to find a rational basis for resolving all such quibbles. The exact definition is unimportant; what is important is its relation to other economic concepts that have similarly fuzzy edges.

The key concept is *externalities*. An externality occurs whenever an action taken by some economic unit has a *direct* impact on the welfare or productivity of some other economic unit. Usage of this term is not exactly uniform in the literature in a couple of respects, and some confusion has resulted. In the interest of uniformity where it matters, let me call attention to two nebulous aspects. First is the question of reimbursement. My definition did not mention reimbursement, but some

The author is David A. Wells Professor of Political Economy, Harvard University.

definitions require that it be absent.[1] Consider the famous Pigouvian example of the railway whose engines emit sparks that sometimes ignite farmers' fields. There is an externality there by my definition. Furthermore the externality would still be present if the farmer owned the right-of-way and were able to charge the railroad for the privilege of sending an engine past his field. That is where definitions diverge. It seems most useful to say, in this latter case, that there is still an externality but that the price can be set so that the proper (in some sense) amount of it will be generated. In general, I should say, externalities are technological relationships and not matters of law or institutional arrangements. Institutional arrangements are significant because they affect the amount of the externality that is produced, but the externality will be there, paid for or not, unless the offending activity is suspended entirely or the offended people move out of range. Unless we define externalities in this way we are in danger of confusing two fields of discourse—technological and institutional—when we discuss externalities.

The other ambiguity about which I wish to take a position is the distinction between technological and pecuniary externalities. The operative phrase in the definition I proposed as a ground rule is *direct impact*. That definition does not admit effects transmitted via the price mechanism as externalities at all. Though I presume that that position is generally accepted nowadays, pecuniary externalities do survive in the literature. The phrase appears to go back to Viner's authoritative paper on cost curves (9), and in that connection it is interesting to recall what he had to say about the kinds of externalities that concern us: "External technological diseconomies, or increasing technical coefficients of production as output of the industry as a whole is increased, can be theoretically conceived, but it is hard to find convincing illustrations." The world has changed a great deal since 1931.

Those comments should make the concept of externalities sufficiently precise. Any economic unit's behavior can affect the welfare or productivity of others in a vast number of different ways, through altruism, envy, congestion, pollution, and a myriad of other kinds of connection.

---

[1] For example, Mishan: "External effects may be said to arise when relevant effects on production or welfare go wholly or partially unpriced" (7, p. 6). Mishan is explicit about what he means by this; in particular he means to include all cases in which a firm pays a factor of production less than its social value in alternative occupations. This definition includes the draft, hard bargaining, and a host of other market imperfections as sources of externalities, which I find confusing.

6

Sometimes the connection is physical. That is to say, sometimes there is an identifiable physical medium through which the effects of one agent's activities are transmitted to other agents. Such a medium is what I shall mean by a common property resource.

This point of view has some immediate consequences for our discourse. It means that all problems attributable to the misuse or abuse of common property resources are instances of externalities, and the entire theory of externalities applies to them. But the converse is not true. There are externalities that do not involve common property resources, for example, those attributable to altruism and envy, the advantages of living among better-educated people with habits and tastes agreeable to us, and the benefits conferred by the extension of knowledge and the creation of art. All of those are real externalities, but common property resources are not involved, according to my concept, and we shall only imperil a useful, delimited concept if we try to stretch it to cover too wide a range of externalities.

Second, notice that this concept makes no reference to property rights. The private ski slope and the public park confront exactly the same technological problems, and the admission fee or usage-discipline that is right for one is right for the other. They are classified identically according to this concept, as seems sensible. In Garrett Hardin's now-classic parable (5), the commons is a common property resource, but would remain so if the lord of the manor appropriated it and charged a grazing fee per head. The distinguishing feature of a common property resource is that it transmits influences directly from one economic agent to another. It may, legally, be private property.

At this juncture I must digress briefly onto the topic of property, which has become part of this literature under the well-merited influence of Ronald Coase. It seems to me that much of the literature is confusing, and even wrong, when it discusses the relationship between property rights and the use of common property resources. It is often said that the difficulties arise either because there are no property rights or because they are ill defined. Typically, nothing could be further from the truth. In Garrett Hardin's case, every properly certified member of the village had a perfectly clear entitlement to graze his livestock on the common, and it was enforceable at law. In the famous Pigou-Coase railway example, also, the rights of the participants are clearly defined although, as Coase is at pains to point out, they are not exactly what Pigou assumed them to be (2, sec. VIII). The same is true of fisheries, aquifers, and oil pools, all of which have been used to illustrate gaps

7

in the definition of rights. But there are no gaps in these instances; on the contrary, there are overlaps. Several people have clearly established rights that, when exercised, turn out to be incompatible. I believe that lawyers call this kind of situation a "conflict of rights," and it is far from rare. When it comes to the surface, the courts must decide which right is to prevail. Once the precedent is set, it has the effect of redefining the rights so that they are no longer in conflict. But the point is that clear rights existed before the precedent, and the conflict arose, not from any deficiency of rights or definition, but rather from a superfluity of them. And so it is with common property resources: there are too many rights to them, and when exercised, the rights impair each other.

We come out of this terminological excursion with the conclusion that a common property resource is a kind of public good with the peculiarities that it cannot be augmented, but it can be saturated. It is not easy to say precisely what that means because it is not easy to say precisely what is meant by *using a public good* and because the ways in which users of a public good affect each other are so varied. Let me mention a few examples to remind you of the possibilities.

First there is the oil-pool kind of problem. Each person with access to the pool is under an incentive to withdraw all the oil he can as quickly as he can, before his neighbor does the same. He knows that by drilling and operating superfluous wells he is expending resources without increasing the ultimate yield of the pool; indeed he is likely to diminish it, but he does so all the same. In this case the users do not affect each other at all in the short run, and even if they did not affect the total yield in the long run, the problem would remain.

The fisheries kind of problem is somewhat different. The yield on any day displays diminishing returns to the total amount of fishing effort, so each trawler reduces the productivity of all the others present on the same fishing grounds. In addition, the catch on any day increases the cost of the catch on subsequent days, and the catch in any season impairs the productivity of the grounds in future seasons. There are both short-run and long-run interferences.

In both these examples the mode of damage to the common property resource is the removal of something of value from it, in one case something that regenerates, in the other something that does not. But that is far from the only mode of mutual interference. On the overcrowded beach or congested highway the individual user does not remove anything from the common property resource or change it physically in any way. The mere fact that he is using it is enough to impair its serviceability to others.

Air pollution is quite different again. Here the mode of impairment is the addition of something deleterious to the common property resource. There are short-run effects, and there may be long-run or even permanent effects also.

In all these instances the interferences are reciprocal; each user affects all the others in much the same way. But that need not be the case; the externalities generated by use may be unidirectional. This is so, for example, when birdwatchers and hunters use the same wilderness area or when tanneries and swimmers use the same river.

Now it does not seem possible for a single theoretical formulation to encompass all these modes of interaction: the abstraction of exhaustible components or self-replenishing ones, the insertion of noxious ingredients, mere congestion, and variants of all these. *Common property resources* seems to be a catchall concept for a variety of essentially different circumstances that require different definitions and formulations. The one common element seems to be the presence of numerous users, or of decentralized decision making subject to a shared constraint.

In this circumstance, instead of striving for a general formulation or an exhaustive taxonomy, it seems best to bring out the issues that arise and the possibilities for analysis by examining a series of special cases, and that is what I plan to do.

In all these cases I shall emphasize the distinction between socially optimal or socially efficient behavior, on the one hand, and equilibrium behavior on the other. This is always an important distinction in economic analysis. Where there are no externalities or market imperfections, these two sorts of behavior turn out to be the same, thanks to the skill of the invisible hand. When externalities are present, the equilibrium and the social optimum tend to diverge unless some corrective action is taken, as is well known and as we shall see exemplified repeatedly in what follows. One type of corrective social action, often practically useful and always conceptually illuminating, is to assess some appropriate charges on externality-creating behavior so as to restore the efficacy of the invisible hand. These brief analyses will pay special attention to the existence and characteristics of such corrective charges.

My first case is Garrett Hardin's famous and moving parable of the commons (5). The story is too simple and familiar to need retelling. In essence, there are some herdsmen who share a commons. Each one

9

gains in proportion to the size of his own herd and ignores the collective effects of overgrazing. As a result, Hardin tells us,

the rational herdsman concludes that the only sensible course for him to pursue is to add another animal to his herd. And another; and another. . . . But this is the conclusion reached by each and every rational herdsman sharing a commons. Therein is the tragedy. Each man is locked into a system that compels him to increase his herd without limit—in a world that is limited. Ruin is the destination toward which all men rush, each pursuing his own best interest in a society that believes in the freedom of the commons. (5, p. 1244)

That is very plausible, and surely there is some truth it it. But wherein is the tragedy? Hardin has rushed on toward his grim conclusion too swiftly to make that clear; I want to take it a good deal more slowly.

One possible interpretation is the following. Let $p(X)$ be the probability that an animal will survive to be marketed when the total herd sharing the commons is X. Then the socially optimal size of herd is the one that maximizes $Xp(X)$. We are tempted to rush right in, compute the derivative, and show that the independent herdsmen will try to graze ruinously many cattle. But things are not necessarily that bad. It might be, for example, that

$$p(X) = \frac{a+1}{a+X}, \, a \geq 0,$$

so that the probability of survival is a certainty if a lone animal is grazed, and falls harmonically toward zero for larger herds. If that be the case,

$$\frac{d}{dX} Xp(X) = \frac{a(a+1)}{(a+X)^2} > 0.$$

There is no "tragedy."[2] The size of the marketable herd is an always-increasing function of the number of cattle grazed, and the invisible hand of self-interest leads the herdsmen in the optimal direction. Things are more complicated than Hardin told us. To produce a real tragedy, or even a serious misallocation of resources, from decentralized use of a common property resource, we must introduce additional considerations.

[2] Not in the usual sense, that is. Hardin uses the word in a different sense, to mean "the solemnity of the remorseless working of things" (5, p. 1244). In this sense there is a tragedy, but it is a beneficent one.

It will not even suffice to assume that the carrying capacity of the commons is finite (as Hardin probably does.)[3] Substantially stronger assumptions are needed. One that will suffice is that after some point the marginal productivity of cattle is negative, i.e., that the addition of animals to the herd will actually reduce the number that survives to be marketed. Another line of argument that would buttress Hardin's point is to assume that there is some other scarce resource that is wasted when too many cattle are grazed on the limited commons. For example, the cattle may need tending, or water may be in short supply. Then grazing too many cattle will waste this cooperating resource, even though the carrying capacity of the commons is not reached. In short, the model can be saved by taking other economic considerations into account, but as it stands it is too simple to establish its main conclusion.

My second case follows the route of introducing a second factor, namely labor. Let the commons be a berry patch in which the number of bushels picked on any day shows diminishing returns to the number of person-hours devoted to picking. If $F(X)$ is the number of bushels picked in X person-hours, then the social optimum is attained when $pF(X) - wX$ is maximized. (The definitions of the symbols are conventional.) But none of the individual pickers is concerned about the social optimum. Each is concerned with his own net gain, which we write for the ith picker:

$$pf(x_i, X) - wx_i.$$

In this notation x_i is the number of person-hours spent by the ith picker, and his individual production function, the same for all pickers, shows that his harvest depends both on his own effort (positively) and on the total effort, $X = \Sigma x_i$ (negatively). Furthermore, the individual production functions are related to the aggregate production function by

$$\sum_i f(x_i, X) = F(X).$$

It can be shown that the only function that satisfies this relation and the side-condition $f(0, X) = 0$ (no hours, no berries) is the linear one

$$f(x_i, X) = \frac{x_i}{X} F(X).$$

[3] If the carrying capacity of the commons is finite, the marginal productivity of cattle must approach zero rapidly after some point. In more concrete terms, the addition of one more animal to the herd must, after some point, increase the expected number of premature deaths by virtually unity.

11

This entails that if $pF(X)/X > w$, the individual pickers will spend more time, and additional pickers will be attracted to the field. If the inequality is reversed, usage will shrink. Equilibrium requires exact equality. The equilibrium condition $pF(X)/X = w$ is sufficient to determine X (at a level that is greater than the social optimum), but the x_i remain indeterminate, just as in ordinary competitive models with constant returns to scale.[4]

An immediate moral to be drawn from this simple case is that the frequent and natural assumption—that the aggregate yield from a common property resource depends only on the aggregate use made of it—is very stringent. In particular, it entails that each user's production function has strictly constant returns to scale.

It is well known that the users of the common property resource can be induced to use it to an optimal extent by imposing either a user charge on their labor or a royalty on their harvests. The appropriate user charge in this case is

price x [average product − marginal product]

per person-hour, both products computed from $F(X)$. The corresponding royalty is

price x [1 − elasticity of $F(X)$]

per bushel. The two instruments lead to identical results because of the postulated rigidity of the individual production functions. Whichever device is used, the level of the unit impost that maximizes the net social product also maximizes the aggregate of fees collected. In fact, the two are the same: the optimal charge simply imputes the total net product as rent on the common property resource.

If institutional arrangements permit fairly frequent revision of the royalty rate or user charge, the socially optimal rates can be found by trial and error even if the production function, $F(X)$, is not known.

There are, I think, some real situations—not only berry picking—to which this formulation applies. To be sure, there are few or no produc-

---

[4] I believe that this formulation is the same as Cheung's fishery model (1), but he purports to determine the x_i. The divergence arises from the fact that in Cheung's version each user regards all alien x_i as fixed when choosing his own value (a Chamberlinian assumption), while in mine, each user simply disregards the effect of his choice on the aggregate. Cheung's assumption is more appropriate for small-group problems, mine for large.

tion processes in which a common property resource is combined with only a single private resource, but some consumption processes, particularly recreational ones, are like that. Besides, this model does not really depend on the singleness of the private resource but, rather, on the absence of possibilities for substitution among private resources. Therefore, any sufficiently rigid production situation can be analyzed by this model—in particular, any situation with fixed coefficients of production.

We must now consider the new features that appear when there are possibilities for substitution among private resources that affect the productivity of the common property resource. It will be sufficient to consider the case where there are just two privately provided resources.

Things are sophisticated enough now that instead of telling a story, I shall just set forth a formal model. Suppose, then, that there are n firms (or other users) that share a common property resource. They all produce the same product and have the same production function that uses as inputs two private resources and the common property resource. To be specific, the rate of output (or satisfaction) of the ith user is

$$Y_i = f(x_{1i}, x_{2i}, X_1, X_2, Y, A).$$

In this notation, x_{1i} and x_{2i} are the amounts of the two cooperating resources employed by the ith user, X_1 and X_2 are the total amounts of those resources applied by all users, Y is the total output, and A is the amount of the common property resource. We assume that $f(\quad)$ has positive partial derivatives with respect to x_{1i}, x_{2i}, and A, and zero or negative partials with respect to the other three variables. Furthermore, we assume that $f(\quad)$ is homogeneous of first order with respect to x_{1i} and x_{2i}, so that each user operates under constant returns to scale as far as its private decisions are concerned, and is homogeneous of zeroth order with respect to X_1, X_2, Y, and A. This last assumption means that the output of the individual firm would not be affected if total usage and availability of the common property resource were increased in the same proportion. This is only a virtual condition on the functional form, of course, since by hypothesis the availability of the common property resource cannot be changed. This formulation seems to catch the essence of the fisheries type of situation (apart from long-run considerations) and many others, but it is far from general. It does represent a considerable loosening-up from the previous case, since total output is now

$$Y = \sum_i f(x_{1i}, x_{2i}, X_1, X_2, Y, A)$$

13

and depends on the distribution of inputs among firms as well as on their total.

The common property resource is most efficiently utilized when $pY - w_1X_1 - w_2X_2$ is as great as possible. The uninstructed, independent decisions of the users will not attain this result since each user, quite sensibly, ignores the effect of his decisions on the aggregate arguments. But, as is well known, properly chosen royalties and use charges (r, c_1, c_2, say) can guide the individual users to the social optimum. By straightforward algebra, one such schedule is found to be

$$ r = p \, \frac{\sum_i \frac{\partial f^i}{\partial Y}}{\sum_i \frac{\partial f^i}{\partial Y} - 1} $$

$$ c_1 = -(p - r) \sum_i \frac{\partial f^i}{\partial X_1} $$

$$ c_2 = -(p - r) \sum_i \frac{\partial f^i}{\partial X_2} $$

where the symbol f^i indicates that the partial derivative is to be evaluated with the variables for the ith user at their optimal values.

There are actually more instrument variables in this solution than are needed. The royalty can be set at any desired level less than p (including zero), and the input charges can be adjusted according to a rather messy formula to take up the slack. The formula given is the simplest one mathematically, though not necessarily administratively. Though the use of a royalty is optional and the rate somewhat arbitrary, the charges for the use of complementary inputs are not. They must be set in proportion to the relative marginal damage inflicted on the common property resource, damage being measured in terms of its ability to support production.

Whichever optimal schedule of royalties and user charges is used, it turns out that the total collections just absorb the total net value produced, as a consequence of the homogeneity assumptions. Therefore, maximizing collections or rents is equivalent to maximizing net social product. In contrast to the previous, simpler case, there are now so many variables that it does not seem conceivable that the social optimum can be found by trial and error. Pretty fair estimates of the production technology and of the effects of the externality variables are needed for setting the appropriate charges.

14

Institutionally, this setup corresponds to some real situations but ignores some important possibilities. In terms of our catalog of possible modes of interaction, the cases of pure congestion and of removal of valuable ingredients from the common property resource are covered, with Y as the predominant or sole carrier of the interactions.[5] The case of the insertion of noxious ingredients is also covered to the extent that the quantities introduced are fully determined by the quantities of cooperating factors used. This rules out the possibility of end-of-pipe treatment, which is an important possibility in practice. The range of applicability of this formulation is pretty much the same as that of the various process weight formulas used for environmental regulation.

It should be noted that the production function on which this formulation is based,

$$f(x_{1i}, x_{2i}, X_1, X_2, Y, A),$$

contains three classes of variables: privately determined variables (x_{1i} and x_{2i}), externality-carriers (X_1, X_2, Y), and the quantity of the common property resource or public good (A). The privately determined variables are chosen so as to maximize the attainment of private objectives. The externality-carriers are by-products or functions of the privately determined variables and are not independently determined. The amount of the common property resource is determined exogenously to the system.

This classification is characteristic of a much wider range of externality or public goods problems and displays the way in which the generation of externalities interacts with the available quantities of shared resources.

The approach just illustrated can be generalized, on a formal level, to incorporate the possibility of end-of-pipe treatment. One need only write the basic production function as

$$f(x_{1i}, x_{2i}, u_i, U, Y, A),$$

---

[5] Here I should make explicit some terminological distinctions that help to keep thinking straight. Some goods have the property that their production or use creates externalities. I call these *externality-conveyors* or *externality-carriers*, and distinguish them from *externalities* per se. Thus gasoline is an externality-carrier; the associated externalities are the increase in average travel time and the smarting eyes, bronchial complaints, and so on caused by the widespread use of gasoline. An externality-conveyor is also distinguished from the medium or common property resource through which it conveys, just as a ship is distinguished from an ocean.

u_i could be $u_i(x_{1i}, x_{2i}, x_{3i})$

clean up

where u_i (perhaps a vector) measures the impact of the ith user on the common property resource and U is the sum or some other symmetric function of the u_i. The previous formulation is a special case of this one. Straightforward mathematics will disclose the optimal levels of all variables as well as the scheme of royalties and charges that will induce the users to select those optimal levels. There are no surprises or new insights to be found by so doing, and I shall not go through the formalities. Besides, when waste treatment comes into the picture, the assumption of constant returns to scale becomes especially unpalatable since increasing returns are a notorious feature of treatment plants of nearly all types. In short, we are now reaching the level of abstraction at which it seems best to turn back to ad hoc, special-purpose models that take advantage of the special features of special situations.

Let me call attention to the fact that all the models I have analyzed are stationary equilibrium models. They do not apply at all to the oil-pool kind of problem or any problem in which resource exhaustion is a significant feature. They apply to fisheries-type problems only to the extent that depletion of the breeding stock can be ignored. To contend with problems of those classes, it is necessary to introduce considerations derived from capital theory.

The most elegant treatments that I know of the economics of depletable resources are those of Hotelling (6) and Weinstein and Zeckhauser (10). Neither, unfortunately, deals with the common-pool aspect of the problem. In the following, I use a simplification of the Weinstein-Zeckhauser analysis as a point of departure.

Consider an oil pool with multiple users. At any moment there are S barrels of oil in the pool. The total cost of extracting oil at the rate of y barrels per year is $C(y, S)$, and, for given y, increases as the underground stock is drawn down. In fact, I want it to increase so rapidly that it climbs toward infinity while there is still some oil left. This device is not only realistic; it frees us from having to worry about terminal constraints on the total amount to be withdrawn over time.

On the demand side, we assume that the demand curve for oil from this pool is constant over time. The area under the demand curve to the left of the current rate of withdrawal is $D(y)$, and this represents the gross social value of that rate of withdrawal. The current price at any moment is then $p = D'(y)$.

At any moment the rate of net social benefit from the operation of the pool is $D(y) - C(y, S)$. Therefore, using a discount rate of r, the optimal time-path of withdrawals is the one that maximizes

$$\int_0^\infty e^{-rt} \, [D(y) - C(y, \, S)] dt,$$

taking account of the fact that each moment's withdrawal reduces the stock in the pool—$dS/dt = -y$—and therefore increases the cost of extraction forever in the future. This is a standard control theory problem. The necessary condition for an optimal time-path is that there exist a shadow-price variable, $u(t)$, such that at every moment when $y > 0$

$$p - C_1(y, \, S) - u(t) = 0$$

and

$$\frac{du}{dt} - ru = C_2(y, \, S).$$

These laws of motion determine the time-paths of y, S, p, and u when oil is extracted at the socially optimal rate. The first of them identifies the shadow-price with the marginal net profit per barrel. The second shows how the marginal net profit changes over time as the stock of oil is drawn down. In fact, integrating the second law, it can be seen that

$$u(t) = -\int_t^\infty e^{-r(z-t)} C_2(y, \, S) dz,$$

which is the present value at time t of the marginal increases in extraction costs over all time entailed by a marginal increase in the rate of output at time t.

So far we have not even mentioned the common-pool aspect of the problem which is our main concern, but we can do so now. The individual oil well operator is motivated by the value of $u(t)$ at present and in the future. If $u(t)$ is increasing faster than the rate of interest, he can maximize his wealth by not extracting oil now, but waiting until the future when it will be more profitable to do so. Contrariwise, if the rate of interest is greater than the rate of growth of $u(t)$, he is best advised to withdraw all he can right now and invest the net proceeds at the current rate of interest (the individual owner ignores the future increase in costs that he imposes on everyone by drawing down S). He will be induced to extract a positive finite quantity only when the marginal profitability of withdrawals grows at a rate just equal to the current rate of interest. The proper inducement can be provided by imposing a unit withdrawal tax or royalty equal to $u(t)$. Then the after-tax net marginal

17

profits will grow at the rate r, and the operators will be content to withdraw oil at the socially optimal rate.

Thus the oil-pool problem leads to the same kind of conclusion that we reached in the static cases. The charges that induce efficient individual behavior are those that absorb the total net rent attainable from using the common property resource, and are maximized when those net rents are maximized. Similar conclusions apply to the somewhat more complicated problems of partially depletable resources, as in the fisheries case.

All the preceding models were symmetric: all the participants were similarly placed and suffered reciprocally from each other's use of the common property resource. We turn now to asymmetric problems— those in which some users impose external costs on others while receiving none (or very different ones) in return. The asymmetry introduces a range of new, intriguing, and very difficult problems, namely those relating to equity and distributional considerations.

Distributional considerations are not entirely absent from the symmetric-use problems, of course. In the foregoing cases we simply took it for granted that the proceeds of the charges, royalties, or whatnot were redistributed to the users of the common property resource in such a way that all benefited, which is not difficult to achieve since those charges enhance the productivity of the resource. The formula for redistribution can give rise to lively disagreement, the more vociferous in proportion as the situation departs from exact symmetry. For symmetry is a powerful solvent of disagreements; people tend to sympathize with the claims and problems of others in proportion as they are in the same situation. Now we must confront the kind of problem that arises when this close bond of human sympathy is stretched.

There is another marked difference between the symmetric and asymmetric cases. In the symmetric cases, all users of the common property resource suffer from uninstructed individualistic use. In fact, individualistic use is not even technologically efficient. For in those cases the common property resource is used to produce some relatively homogeneous product (which may be a particular kind of consumer satisfaction), whose total amount is actually diminished if externalities are ignored. An unambiguous improvement is achieved by imposing or inducing moderation, insofar as more is better.

The situation is otherwise in asymmetric cases. There, more downstream output can be attained only at the expense of less, or less economical, upstream output. Uninstructed use can be on the production possibility frontier, and the social waste, if any, is to that extent more subtle and more difficult to measure.

The philosopher's stone for all such problems is the social welfare function, but the philosopher's stone has yet to be found. Failing that helpful aid, the fall-back position is Pareto-optimality, admittedly a modest aspiration level just because it evades questions of equity and distributional wisdom. But even Pareto-optimality is not a clearly defined test, especially in the context of common property resources. We say that a situation is Pareto-optimal if it cannot be altered without harming at least one person, but we do not say what constraints have to be honored in considering various possibilities for alteration. Suppose, for example, that if an upstream user spent $1,000 more on effluent treatment, downstream productivity would be increased by many times that amount, but that there is no socially sanctioned method by which he can be reimbursed. Is the current situation Pareto-optimal? I know of no authoritative answer to that question. The current situation does fail the compensation tests. Nevertheless, I should say that it is Pareto-optimal, because I regard social constraints as being just as genuine and immutable as physical constraints. Both kinds can change over time, and on the whole, physical constraints have proved to be more flexible than social and institutional ones. So I shall regard a situation as Pareto-optimal, even if it fails the compensation tests, if there is no socially acceptable way to compensate losers for a change that benefits others.

This brings us back to our earlier discussion of "conflict of rights." If we impose some restraint on an upstream user, we impair his recognized rights. If we compensate him by imposing a charge on downstream beneficiaries, then we are taxing them for the mere exercise of their legitimate rights. Whether we compensate or not we affront someone who is likely to be justifiably adamant about the inviolability of his rights. What should be done in such a pickle?

I have already said, in part. In individual cases the parties go to court, and the court decides, on the legalistic grounds that courts employ, whose right is genuine and whose is spurious. Economists have a role to play in such legal determinations. As Coase (2) documents, the courts often take economic costs and benefits into account in resolving conflicts of rights. Economists can therefore contribute by estimating those quantities. Fortunately for us, we do not have to make the final determination of whose benefits should preponderate over whose costs.

Once the court has decided, it may be possible to arrange compensation without infringing anyone's rights; if so, the compensation test applies. The result of this test is to maximize to all users the aggregate value of using the common property resource.

But that is not the usual or most important way to resolve conflicts of rights to the use of a common property resource. The most important way is to redefine those rights by legislative enactment. Here, for example, lie the roots of one of the arguments against the concept of effluent fees. It is said that they are "licenses to pollute," and thus confer a right that the opponents regard as altogether dubious. I desist from entering that debate, which I have mentioned only by way of illustration.

Now, an economist is well advised to avoid making pronouncements about who has the right to do what, and to whom, but he cannot evade the responsibility for offering whatever illumination economics can shed on the consequences of various allocations of rights. For example, the Federal Water Pollution Control Amendments of 1972 gave primacy to the rights of those who like unpolluted water over the rights of those who use public waters for the discharge of wastes.[6] Economic analysis has some light to shed on the wisdom of this assignment of rights.

On the other hand, this determination having been made, it is bootless to reexamine the question in the context of particular watersheds. From now on, until further notice, the right to clean water has to be regarded as an operative constraint in estimating Pareto-optimal possibilities for utilizing public waters. This means that any plan of use that impairs the quality of the water has to include adequate compensation to downstream riparians.

On these grounds, I conclude that the economist working on problems relating to common property resources need not confront the unsolvable problems of distributional equity. He can accept the inherited assignment of rights as establishing the comparative levels of welfare to which the various users of the resource are entitled and can devote himself to

[6] Federal Water Pollution Control Amendments is a very complicated document, and my interpretation is open to some question. The interpretation in the text is derived from the statements of congressional intent to the effect that ultimately public waters shall be returned to their unpolluted state and that, pending that happy day, no public waters shall have their qualities degraded below their current levels. The operative sections of the law, however, are much less ambitious. They require only that in the near future effluents be subjected to "best practical" treatment and that in the intermediate future "best available" treatment be applied. The phrases in quotation marks are subject to administrative definition, and nowhere does the act reconcile them with the high aspiration level of the statement of intent. It seems to be assumed that "best available" will eventually be defined in a way that is consistent with the stated goals of the act.

ascertaining the most efficient way to utilize the resource while respecting this constraint.

I have taken the position that the practicing economist is not equipped or obligated to adjudicate rights and equities. On the other hand, he is virtually forced to make judgments about political feasibility. The reason is that political expediency is a dominant—and proper, in my opinion—consideration in decisions concerning the use and development of common property resources. Economic analyses that lead to recommendations that flout political expediency are simply wasted, and the more skillful the analysis, the more lamentable the waste. To avoid squandering our efforts on such enterprises, we must design our analyses to recognize political constraints along with all the others. In some circumstances, at least, a decision has to be accepted as Pareto-optimal if all the possibilities that seem superior on strictly economic grounds are politically impracticable.

I have a modest proposal for incorporating political considerations. This proposal takes off from a variant of "multiobjective programming." The variation consists in considering as the outputs obtained from a common property resource, not qualitatively different commodities or services, but the contribution to the welfares of different, relatively homogeneous groups of citizens. Taking this point of view, suppose that there are a finite number of alternatives for managing some common property resource. Then we can construct a table, or matrix, with a column for each alternative and a row for each class of citizens to be considered. The entries consist in the changes in the welfares of the row citizens that would result from adopting the column alternatives. Since the various alternatives generally cost money (or real resources) and there are options as to how the financial burden is to be distributed, an additional row is needed for the joint or initially unallocated costs of the alternatives.

Such a table may disclose at once that certain alternatives are inadmissible, using the word in the usual sense that an alternative is inadmissible if there is some other one that costs no more on the joint cost row, that enhances the welfare of every group at least as much, and that enhances the welfare of some group more. This is a weak test, however, and most sensible alternatives will survive it.

To obtain a more powerful principle of discrimination, we revert to the joint cost row and recognize that these costs must be assessed against the benefiting groups in some manner, reducing their welfares thereby. Now I can state a theorem that is virtually obvious intuitively:

21

Consider two alternatives and suppose that the sum of the group net benefit entries for Alternative No. 1 minus its joint cost is greater than the same quantity computed for Alternative No. 2. Then no matter how the joint costs of Alternative No. 2 are assessed among the beneficiaries, there will be some way of assessing the costs of Alternative No. 1 so that every group is better off with Alternative No. 1 (so assessed) than with Alternative No. 2 (so assessed).

This theorem extends immediately to any finite number of alternatives. If the sum of group net benefits minus joint costs is greater for Alternative No. 1 than for any other alternative, then no matter which other alternative is chosen and how its joint costs are allocated, there is a way to allocate the costs of Alternative No. 1 that makes every group better off.

In a sense, then, Alternative No. 1 is dominant in these circumstances. Notice that this is a restricted version of the usual compensation test, since reallocating joint costs is a restricted and somewhat devious form of compensation. Notice, more particularly, that the various allocations of welfare attainable by adopting Alternative No. 1 and allocating its costs in some manner satisfy the von Neumann-Morgenstern definition of a solution to an N-person game. So we can invoke the entire literature of N-person game theory to both justify and criticize the claim that an alternative like Alternative No. 1 of the theorems has a special plausibility and interest. I can summarize that literature by saying that von Neumann-Morgenstern solutions do have a strong intuitive attraction, but that on moderately close inspection they are not very compelling. They are, however, the most nearly satisfying solutions for such situations that anyone has proposed thus far.

Let me recall some of the characteristics of von Neumann-Morgenstern solutions that lead to this qualified advocacy. On the favorable side, we have seen that they are efficient economically in the narrow sense that the excess of total benefits over costs, to whomsoever they may accrue, is greater for outcomes in the solution than for any others. For this reason, the economist who recommends the alternative that generates the solution set is in a strong position. Whatever other alternative may be proposed, he can suggest a cost allocation based on his proposal that will confer greater net benefits on everybody. He even has something to say about how the costs of the favored alternative should be allocated—namely, so as to placate potential opponents by giving them about as much net welfare gain as they could hope to obtain by any expedient. So the alternative chosen by this simple (and conventional) test has much to recommend it.

To see the salient weakness of the solution concept, we must recognize that neither in politics nor in game theory is unanimity required for a decision. Now, given any outcome in the solution set (that is, a management alternative together with an allocation of its joint cost), it is quite possible for there to be an outcome outside the set that is preferred by a politically effective plurality. The only rejoinder to such an objection is that there must be some other outcome in the solution set that will be preferable to the outside one from everybody's point of view. But, alas, this third outcome need not be preferred to the first one by any politically effective grouping or coalition. To restate: Any outcome in the solution set may be defeated politically by some outside outcome, but that outside outcome in turn can be defeated by some other outcome inside the set which, in its turn, may be defeated by some other outside outcome. And so on forever. Such are the caprices of lack of transitivity.

Now we have opened the door to the full richness and confusion of N-person game theory: coalition formation, characteristic functions, and all the rest. We shall not go through that door, however, after this glance inside. Instead, I have to point out that the application of game theory to the management of common property resources is more complicated than I may have suggested.

The two key theorems that I presented are not really applicable in that simple form to most actual common property resource problems. The reason is that those theorems, and all similar theorems, depend on the ability to make side-payments either explicitly or implicitly. In common property resource problems, under current institutional conditions, the scope for side-payments is limited to the range of choice for allocating the joint costs. If the joint costs are small or nil, there will be very little room for maneuver.[7] Besides, even if the joint costs are large in toto, the ability to allocate them strategically is confined by legal and

---

[7] Lest I appear to contradict the theorems, I have to mention that the proofs require the possibility of negative cost allocations in some situations, since the net benefits conferred on some group by an outcome outside the solution set may be so much greater than those conferred by the alternative generating the set that, even if that group bore none of the costs, it would still be worse off than under the outside outcome. I recently came across just such a situation. The optimal alternative happened to be disastrous for a decisive group. They had to be assigned a negative share of the costs to make it acceptable to them and, by an artful adaptation of what was legally and politically possible, this was arranged. So negative cost shares are more than a mathematical figment.

institutional limitations on the taxes and other instruments that have to be used.

This complication means that conventional game theory needs some modification before being applied to common property resource problems and similar problems of public decisions. The essential modification required is to recognize that, whereas in game theory as usually presented a coalition wins a specified total of resources which it can distribute among its members as it wills, in these applications a coalition wins access to a specified and limited set of distributions of individual gains, from which it can choose. In technical language, the characteristic function—conventionally denoted by $v(S)$—has to be regarded as a set of attainable distributions rather than as a simple scalar sum. This modification has been dealt with to some extent in the literature and leads to a theory similar to the familiar one, but somewhat weaker. But this it not the place to pursue so specialized a topic.

The elaboration of game theory to take account of restrictions on side-payments is intriguing intellectually but, I suspect, not very important practically. At the Environmental Systems Program we are beginning to build a small inventory of documented case studies of political decisions about environmental matters. It is still too fragmentary to permit reliable inferences, but so far we have found only a small minority of instances in which it can be suspected that limitations on side-payments prevented the adoption of an economically efficient plan, and in no instance have we found that those limitations were clearly inhibiting. Moreover, we have found that it is very difficult to ascertain just what the limitations are in any instance. The situation is analogous to that found in applications of linear programming to production problems, where ingenious and highly motivated businessmen have a tendency to discover "activities" that the more disinterested analysts do not foresee when constructing their matrices. Just so, in environmental decision problems, the people actually concerned display extraordinary resourcefulness in discovering expedients that permit the allocation of costs needed to effectuate the decision that they want. I won't go so far as to say that in practice there are no limitations on attainable cost allocations, but will say that those limits are generally so flexible that disregarding them is a fair approximation in practice.

Throughout this extensive review of analytic techniques applicable to decisions about common property resources, I have never gotten to a number of very important technical matters. It is a far cry from any of the models that I have sketched to numerical models that can be applied to real decision problems by simulation or other means. The chasm is not just computational; it contains real conceptual difficulties such as how to allow for uncertainty, how to find relevant rates of discount for time streams of costs and benefits, how to value and compare benefits and costs that cannot be reduced readily to monetary equivalents. All those are respectable obstacles that must be surmounted in crossing the chasm. But I have elected to stay on the theoretical side of the gorge on the grounds that those very important issues are nonetheless one step removed from the main business of this conference, which is what principles should guide decisions about the use of common property resources after all the technical problems of gathering data and analyzing their implications have been surmounted.

REFERENCES

1. Cheung, Steven N. S. "The Structure of a Contract and the Theory of a Nonexclusive Resource," *Journal of Law and Economics*, vol. 13 (April 1970), pp. 49–70.
2. Coase, Ronald. "The Problem of Social Cost," *Journal of Law and Economics*, vol. 3 (October 1960), pp. 1–44.
3. Dales, J. H. *Pollution, Property and Prices.* Toronto: University of Toronto Press, 1968.
4. Freeman, A. Myrick, III, and Haveman, Robert H. "Clean Rhetoric and Dirty Water," *The Public Interest*, vol. 7 (Summer 1972), pp. 51–65.
5. Hardin, Garrett. "The Tragedy of the Commons," *Science*, vol. 162 (December 13, 1968), pp. 1243–48.
6. Hotelling, Harold. "The Economics of Exhaustible Resources," *Journal of Political Economy*, vol. 39 (April 1931), pp. 137–75.
7. Mishan, E. J. "Reflections on Recent Developments in the Concept of External Effects," *Canadian Journal of Economics and Political Science*, vol. 31, no. 1 (February 1965), pp. 1–34.
8. Ruff, Larry E. "The Economic Common Sense of Pollution," *The Public Interest*, vol. 5 (Spring 1970), pp. 69–85.
9. Viner, Jacob. "Cost Curves and Supply Curves," *Zeitschrift für Nationalökonomie*, 1931.
10. Weinstein, Milton C., and Zeckhauser, Richard J. "The Optimal Consumption of Depletable Natural Resources." John F. Kennedy School of Government Discussion Paper No. 13A. Cambridge, Mass.: Harvard University, August 1972. Processed.

CLIFFORD S. RUSSELL

Comment

I FOUND Dorfman's paper a superb piece of exposition in the tradition of his well-known articles on capital theory,[1] linear programming,[2] and control theory.[3] It made sense of a difficult and confusing business and will be useful to many far beyond the confines of this forum.

One charged with discussing such a paper is in a difficult position if he insists on confining his remarks to the content of the piece itself, for there is little with which one can profitably take exception.[4] My solution will be to depart at something of a tangent and concentrate on another aspect of the question of the technical basis for decision making, one closer to my own research interests if not to those of the other forum participants.

For the sake of form, let me take my departure from two related points mentioned by Dorfman:

1. the necessity for ad hoc special-purpose models for the analysis of specific situations (p. 9);

The author is a Research Associate, Resources for the Future, Inc.

[1] "A Graphical Exposition of Böhm-Bawerk's Interest Theory," *REStud*, vol. 26 (February 1959), pp. 153–58; and "Waiting and the Period of Production," *Quarterly Journal of Economics*, vol. 73 (August 1959), pp. 351–72.

[2] "Mathematical or Linear Programming," *American Economic Review*, vol. 43 (December 1953), pp. 797–825.

[3] "An Economic Interpretation of Optimal Control Theory," *American Economic Review*, vol. 59 (December 1969), pp. 817–31.

[4] I do disagree with Dorfman's assertion (p. 6) that the existence of relations usefully called "externalities" is independent of ownership and institutions. There seems a priori to be no reason for breaking with the standard definition, which stresses that externalities are effects *external to individual economic decision-making units*. Indeed, in Dorfman's own paper this departure seems to have nothing to do with the examples. One need only look, for example, at the berry-picking production function to see that a single private owner of a berry bush would have a production function, $F(X)$, which would lead him to an optimal picking decision.

2. the work that has been and is being done at Harvard on Pareto-admissible analysis and the use of multiple-objective function programming (briefly mentioned on p. 21).

These two points touch on the matter of the technical basis for real-world decisions; that is, they raise the question of what economists and social-choice theorists (and engineers and ecologists) can contribute to informing the people who are charged with actually making policy in fields, such as pollution control, where cause and effect may be obscure and the implications of a particular possible policy choice extremely difficult to trace. One would hope that in such fields there would be some alternatives to trial-and-error messing about with the world itself. Ideally, one would like to be able to tell a politician or administrator in advance whether a contemplated policy is physically possible; if it is, what it will mean in terms of ambient environmental quality levels; what it will imply by way of costs; and who, at least in the first instance, will have to pay those costs. Someone, of course, has to make an effort to match the questions the predictive mechanism (the model) is designed to answer, with the questions of interest to the responsible people. And, depending on the forum in which the policy makers operate, such information will have to be presented in one or another way.

In briefest terms, then, there are two major facets to the problem of the technical basis for decision making as I choose to define it:

1. providing some mechanism for predicting the outcomes (in more or less detail) to be expected if particular hypothetical policies are chosen and put into practice;
2. making the mechanism useful to the "client" by feeding him information in a form suitable to the institutional setting in which he finds himself.

In drawing attention to these two facets of the problem, I shall slight a host of complicated questions, just as did Dorfman. In fact, I shall slight all the same questions: for example, how to reflect uncertainty and how to choose a rate of discount to apply to future costs and benefits. Neither shall I deal with some questions peculiar to my own bent: for example, how complicated the mechanisms must be to provide sufficient realism to be persuasive to policy makers; and on the other side of that coin, how complicated the models can become before they are judged too costly, or too difficult computationally, or simply too difficult to understand.

Within this new subject I have set for myself I would like to concentrate on drawing a few distinctions by way of sorting out some of the major strands of research (at least as my biased eyes see them) currently being pursued.

In the construction of the predictive mechanisms the approaches taken may usefully be divided into two groups. The first, I would label the simulation approach. In it, a specific policy is applied directly to a policy instrument (or "handle") as, for example, a discharge limitation applied to a smokestack. The implications of this imposition, such as the resulting ambient concentrations, are then calculated in a recursive manner. Examples of this approach include the ambitious Implementation Planning Program developed by TRW for the Environmental Protection Agency,[5] and a number of the projects funded by the National Science Foundation under the Research Applied to National Needs (RANN) program.[6]

The major advantage of this approach is that the mathematics and computations will not, in general, be problems. Functional relationships between discharge and ambient concentration (or species population) can be as complex as desired by the ecologist. One need not be concerned about convexity or the mechanics of optimization in nonlinear problems.[7] It is also possible that this approach will have more appeal for policy makers who think most easily in terms of a small set of familiar policy handles.

The principal disadvantage of a simulation mechanism is, of course, that it provides no assurance that the same *results*, for example the same levels of ambient quality, could not be achieved more cheaply by another policy. And there is, in general, no systematic way of trying to find such a "better" solution. If the number of policy handles and the positions to which each can be turned are at all numerous, their exhaustive search is clearly going to be very expensive. Regres-

[5] TRW, Inc., "Air Quality Implementation Planning Program," Environmental Protection Agency, November 1970, I and II (also available from National Technical Information Service, Springfield, Virginia, 22151, PB 198 299 and PB 198 300 respectively).

[6] See B. T. Mar and W. T. Newell, *Assessment of Selected RANN Environmental Modeling Efforts*, prepared for the National Science Foundation, June 1973.

[7] Such an approach may include, as does the IPP, a cost minimization subroutine for the individual stacks. It is, however, relatively easy to solve many small, unconnected optimization problems. It is when some constraints are shared—and especially when they are nonlinear—that the serious computational difficulties enter.

sion approaches with random solutions may or may not be useful. There are certainly problems with choosing the functional form for the response surface to be fitted.

The other category of approach I shall refer to as optimization. In this, a policy is applied at the level of the desired results (e.g., a set of maximum acceptable ambient concentrations is specified), and the model finds the "cheapest" policy for meeting it (e.g., the "cheapest" set of discharge standards to be imposed on the region's stacks).[8] This is the approach which I think characterizes the work done at Harvard, RFF, Cornell, Case-Western, and Purdue. The classic example is, of course, the Delaware Estuary Comprehensive Study.[9]

Here the advantages and disadvantages are the opposites of those just discussed under simulation. We trade off mathematical ease for the ability to find more efficient ways to attain given results. In a particular case, the mathematical difficulties connected with optimization may very well come to dominate the other concerns of the model builders; and one must be careful not to claim too much. But it may be healthy to have the discipline of an optimization algorithm imposed on the modeling enterprise. It certainly dampens any desire to try to reproduce the real world inside a digital computer.

In the "old days," when systems modeling was new, the client frequently was a single decision maker within an executive agency, able to be interested in economic efficiency to the exclusion of other considerations (for example, a general responsible for bomber maintenance scheduling in the Strategic Air Command). As these tools have begun to be applied to a broad range of social problems, however, it has been recognized that the new clients are operating in a political framework, and that for them economic efficiency is only one of many relevant criteria. Early failures have stimulated the search for new approaches to the dual problem of structuring the models and conveying the results so that they are of some use to the client—be he legislator or appointed board member, elected or appointed executive.

Let me mention three different means of connecting model and client which are the subject of current research and experimentation. First, some are convinced that role or game playing is the answer. Here,

---

[8] *Cheapest* is put in quotes simply to emphasize that the solution may be subject to other constraints, as for example on how costs may be distributed.

[9] Delaware River Basin Commission, "Final Progress Report: Delaware Estuary and Bay Water Quality Sampling and Mathematical Modeling Project," May 1970.

29

real policy makers are invited to play a computer game with a model of the common property resource management problems under consideration. The players are encouraged to adopt roles other than their own actual role and to explore the feasible space while presumably learning how the other players may react when the game is played in earnest. Possible solutions not apparent to the unaided imagination may be "found" by this interaction of knowledgeable participants.[10] A second approach, developed at Harvard under Dorfman's leadership, involves the exploration of the set of "Pareto-admissible" decisions using an objective function in which the net benefits accruing to various concerned interest groups appear with political weights.[11] The constitutional setting is envisaged as an appointed river basin authority made up of interest group representatives (one from the Society, one from industry, one from municipal government, etc.). Third, our approach at RFF has centered on application of Ed Haefele's work concerning vote trading.[12] Here the institutional setting is assumed to be a regional legislature. The classical efficiency models are restructured to include the possibility of constraining the distribution of cost (as, for example, the increases in home heating bills occasioned by lowering acceptable sulfur contents in distillate heating oil) in addition to the usual physical measures of ambient environmental quality. The complexities of the situation are then explored using a variation on the vote-trading model described by Haefele.[13] The idea here is that the paired models can help the legislators discover mixes of policies which command majority (or more than majority) support—policies which would be difficult for individual legislators to discover on their own

[10] See, for example, Charles Thurow, John Steinhart, and Tom Smith, *W.A.L.R.U.S.: Water and Land Resource Utilization Simulation Player's Manual* (Madison: University of Wisconsin, Sea Grant Program, Wis-SG-73-403, May 1973).

[11] See Robert Dorfman, "Conceptual Model of a Regional Water Quality Authority," in *Models for Managing Regional Water Quality*, edited by Robert Dorfman, Henry Jacoby, and Harold A. Thomas, Jr. (Cambridge, Mass.: Harvard University Press, 1973), chap. 2.

[12] See C. S. Russell, W. O. Spofford, Jr., and E. T. Haefele, "Environmental Quality Management in Metropolitan Areas," presented at the International Economic Association Conference on Urbanization and the Environment, Copenhagen, June 1972.

[13] For example, "Coalitions, Minority Representation and Vote-Trading Probabilities," *Public Choice*, vol. 8 (Spring 1970), pp. 75–90, and "A Utility Theory of Representative Government," *American Economic Review*, vol. 59 (June 1971), pp. 350–67.

because of the difficulty of telling how the desires of a particular district, if written into law, will affect the residents of other districts.

Because I have done some work in both the Dorfman (Harvard) and the Haefele (RFF) modes, I am distressed that there appears to be considerable confusion on all sides about the relation between the two approaches. Accordingly, I would like to spend some additional time in attempting to bring out the parallels and the contrasts between them.

It seems to me that the parallels can most easily be drawn by quoting from statements made by the two groups. Thus, Dorfman, describing his rationale and his goals for the Pareto-admissible approach, writes:[14]

This framework . . . may have practical as well as scientific utility. [It] will indicate, among other things, how various provisions of enabling legislation and charters are likely to influence the performance of local authorities. (p. 44)

In addition . . . [it] may therefore provide some guidance to the staff in acquiring and organizing data relevant to decisions and in reducing them to the most pertinent and vivid form. (p. 44)

In short, one must not view an RBA as a body of governors seeking to discover and implement the general will, but rather as a forum in which the interests of the individuals most concerned are somehow reconciled. (p. 49)

It should be remarked that this view of the RBA as a synthesizer of the goals and objectives of other groups and agencies . . . contradicts the supposition of most analyses of river basin planning. It is much more usual to assume that the RBA arrives at its decisions in the light of some clear-cut objective, such as achieving a stated level of quality at the lowest possible total cost. . . . The conceptual framework that we have just suggested rejects the underlying assumptions of these and all other analytic approaches that depend on maximizing some well defined social objective function. (p. 52)

The justification, of course, is that such a global consequence as the totality of benefits or the aggregate economic cost of a plan is only one of the considerations taken into account by the people who make the decisions, and is not the most prominent consideration for most of the participants. (p. 52)

It should be noted that this model does not simulate or duplicate or in any way supplant other means for arriving at decisions about water quality control. It merely collects and organizes the pertinent data, and predicts that certain initially conceivable decisions will not, in fact, be adopted. (p. 75)

In short, the notion of a government agency that responds to the wishes

[14] Dorfman, "Conceptual Model."

31

of some constituency, rather than one that pursues its own goals, lies at the foundation of this analysis. (p. 77)

The statements made in our IEA paper are strikingly similar and demonstrate the closely parallel nature of our fundamental motivation:[15]

These circumstances have, together with other broader influences, produced what we may call the classical economic and political models for environmental quality management. The classical economic models are designed to find the most efficient configuration of residuals discharges for a region; where efficiency is defined as the minimum sum of damages and abatement costs, when damages are known; or as the minimum abatement cost, when ambient quality standards are imposed. These models are in the tradition of systems analysis, a field which grew up under the protective wing of U.S. government executive agencies, particularly the military departments, in the years after World War II. The models follow the ancestral line; they implicitly or explicitly assume the existence of a decision maker (a person or a "board"), pursuing in a single-minded fashion the objective of economic efficiency; letting the distributional chips fall where they may. . . . (p. 2)

The ideal [has been] to "get politics out" of decision making, i.e., to concentrate on economic efficiency; though the result has simply been to allow the Congress to avoid doing its job, and to shove the "politics" out into the new agencies, where the best organized and financed special interest groups can nearly always win. (p. 3)

It is precisely here, at the exile of traditional politics and the apparent victory of efficiency, that the classical models stumble; and to their failure can be attributed some considerable portion of current disenchantment with our efforts at improving environmental quality. (p. 4)

At the same time, economists and engineers offering their technically reasonable models to these agencies find that their solutions are only acceptable when these solutions agree with the decisions already tacitly made. (p. 4)

Our position is implicit in the above discussion. We believe that the classical political and economic models are inadequate to the task of deciding on a socially desirable balance between residuals discharge (type, quantity, timing and location) and the quality of the air we all breathe, of the landscape we share and of the water courses we use for so many purposes. (p. 5)

In this paper, we suggest that models designed for use by legislatures should be different in some respects from the classical efficiency models. In

[15] Russell, Spofford, and Haefele, "Environmental Quality Management."

particular, a model designed to inform legislative decisions should not condense its "answers" into a single, all-encompassing number, but should provide output showing each legislator what his constituents can expect by way of impacts from any particular policy. That is, the model should ideally show how environmental quality and costs (including such costs as the dislocation of unemployment) are distributed over legislative districts. (p. 5)

Our legislative model is emphatically *not* an attempt to put real legislatures out of business but is simply a device for allowing us to accomplish two things: first, to design the regional model for use in a legislative setting. . . . (p. 6)

Enough, perhaps too much, said about the parallels. Now let us consider the contrasts, and for this purpose I have put together table 1, which summarizes what I take to be the significant differences between the approaches. The reader is free to judge between the two on the basis of his tastes in institutions, his feelings about the desirability and practicality of damage estimation, his stand on vote-trading approaches, or any other grounds. He is equally free to reject both attempts to improve model-client communication. There is, on the other hand, a great deal to be said for a suspension of judgment until more empirical

Table 1. A Brief Table of Contrasts

	Dorfman et al.	*Haefele et al.*
Institutions	River Basin Authority, appointed, interest group representation	Legislature (special or general purpose), elected, geographical representation
Fundamental carrier of political content	Weighted net benefits occurring to interest groups	Preference functions based on constraints on ambient quality and the distribution of costs, over the region's jurisdictions
Mechanism providing information	Sets of Pareto-admissible solutions for imaginable sets of political weights (defined over the interest groups)	"Trades," by which a legislator can impose his key preferences in return for allowing others a similar privilege
Treatment of benefits	Central: qualified assumption that estimation is possible and meaningful	Explicitly left out for public goods: estimation of public good benefits held to be misleading when done as a technical exercise by economists, etc.

33

work is available. It may finally be worth noting that if one accepts the position that damage functions for public bads can be meaningfully estimated, the two approaches appear roughly symmetric in the sense that constraints and objective functions are symmetric in any optimization problem.

ANTHONY C. FISHER & JOHN V. KRUTILLA

Managing the public lands: Assignment of property rights and valuation of resources

THE MANAGEMENT of public lands is becoming an increasingly important, and controversial, problem for a number of reasons. Initially, the lands obtained by grants from the English Crown, by conquest where claims conflicted, and perhaps most notably by the Louisiana and Alaska purchases, were long looked upon as the means by which to advance economic development by selective alienation. This has given rise to many problems in the definition of property rights, to which we shall devote a very substantial part of this paper. But for the moment it can be noted that although these lands were more or less systematically alienated for one or another purpose—subsidizing the construction of railroads, land transfers for purposes of accelerating the development of the West, as in homesteading, and the like—a very large part of the total original lands remain in public ownership. Considering the 2 billion acres in the entire United States, roughly three-quarters of a billion, or a third of the total, remain in public ownership. For comparative purposes, this is larger by a comfortable margin than the area of all the eastern European countries combined and approximately equal to that of the Common Market countries.

The land mass falling under the administrative jurisdiction of the land management agencies in the United States in the aggregate, then, is very considerable and, if efficiently managed, will represent a resource

The authors are Associate Professor of Economics, University of Maryland, and Director, Natural Environments Program, Resources for the Future, Inc., respectively. We are grateful to Talbot Page, Anthony Scott, and Kerry Smith for comments and suggestions on an earlier draft of this material and to Marion Clawson and Robert Dorfman for comments on the forum presentation. This paper is based on the introductory chapters of a longer volume, in manuscript, on the valuation and allocation of natural environmental resources.

of very considerable value. It must be acknowledged, however, that, given the national government's policy of transferring such lands to private ownership as rapidly as possible in order to accelerate economic exploitation, the best of the lands for food and fiber production, for transportation rights-of-way, for energy and mineral exploitation, in short, for extractive and developmental activities promising commercial returns, were transferred long ago. It is true that with continuing advances in technology, previously noncommercial or inaccessible resources are now becoming economic to develop. Nonetheless, the bulk of the lands remaining in public ownership were in one sense or another "passed by." Here we find the vast expanses of arid and semiarid lands in the Southwest; the mountainous regions of the coast, the Cascade-Sierra cordillera, the Rocky Mountains, and the vast mountainous, arctic and subarctic areas of Alaska. Indeed, of the 750 million acres of public lands, approximately a half, until recently, was represented by public lands in Alaska.[1] A large part of the remainder, of no commercial value for food and fiber production, was substantially picked over for minerals since, under the Mining Act of 1872 (just as under the Homestead Act), rights to public lands through patented claims permitted land transfers out of the public domain into private ownership.

The very fact that much of the land, some 18 percent of the coterminous United States and over 50 percent of some of the western states, has remained in public ownership, notwithstanding the public land alienation policy, suggests climatic and topographic conditions that have high recreational and related aesthetic and scientific research values in an affluent society. Indeed, while the Bureau of Land Management, a combination of the old Land Office and the Grazing Service, has as its primary mission the further disposal of public lands, it is at the moment pressing for an organic act to set out its functions, which will be oriented essentially to *land management*, rather than to *land sales*. Moreover, the emphasis on the amenity services which comes through the recent legislation (the Wilderness Act of 1964 and the Wild and Scenic Rivers Act of 1968, the National Trails System Act of 1968, and the various environmental protection acts) will doubtless highlight the management of public lands for amenity as well as

---

[1] The precise situation with respect to the distribution of ownership of lands in Alaska is somewhat uncertain under the current process of land allocations associated with Alaska's somewhat recent transition to statehood.

commodity resources in a manner that was not so much emphasized in the earlier days of public land management. And this is where the rub will be.

It has been noted in the report of the Public Land Law Review Commission (1970) that the public lands have not been particularly well managed precisely in the area where there is a conflict between the production of commodity as compared with amenity resources— i.e., where the production of the former is incompatible with the simultaneous production, or supply of, the latter. While the Public Land Law Review Commission's survey of the problem has been the most systematic and comprehensive, perhaps the activities of the citizen conservation and environmental organizations have been the more publicized. Court actions brought by such groups as the Audubon Society, the Environmental Defense Fund, the Sierra Club and the Wilderness Society are mostly of recent origin and of very great interest from a number of points of view. The citizens' groups are able to obtain injunctions (irrespective of the Environmental Policy Act of 1969) which in effect challenge administrative decisions of such land management agencies as the Forest Service. This ability represents a very remarkable change in the ground rules, first, for citizens dealing with their government, and second, for what is admissible as providing standing in damage suits. That is, the courts appear to be saying that individuals who do not have vested private property rights may nonetheless be regarded as suffering damages incurred from losses through abridgment of continued use of common property resources. The recognition that individuals or groups without vested rights can have standing in damage suits on these matters leads us to consider in more detail the question of property rights on the public lands, and related questions of management.

More specifically, we shall consider (1) the reasons for public ownership or intervention in the allocation and management of the remaining large natural areas, which in turn involves application of the concepts of common property, public goods, and externalities; and (2) the effect of different assignments of property rights on the valuation of these areas and related resources in alternative uses, given that public interest in management calls for some form of benefit-cost analysis. Our results might be characterized briefly and somewhat paradoxically as follows: although the valuation problem could be uniquely resolved by the creation of a market, the resulting allocation would not likely be socially optimal.

PUBLIC LANDS, AND COMMON AND PRIVATE
PROPERTY RESOURCES

The public lands, of course, are owned by the public and are public property in the conventional sense of the term. In law and economics, however, public ownership need not imply that access rights, etc., are obtained or enjoyed in any sense differently from the way they are on private lands. To some extent (depending on technical conditions and policy), public lands are in fact treated as, and reflect the characteristics of, private property resources.

In what sense are public lands managed as private property resources? In the case of private property resources, ownership is vested in an identifiable entity that possesses rights of exclusion, or rights to set the conditions and terms of access to the property or its services. A common property resource, on the other hand, is a resource used, if not necessarily owned, in common by all of the members of the community.[2] Neither exclusion nor discrimination is permitted with respect to its access; it is, therefore, often referred to as an "open-access" resource.

Public lands are not in all cases treated under law and policy as common property resources, however. Uses of the services to which they give rise, or access to the land for the purpose of exploiting its associated resources, are subject to exclusion in some cases. Access to the timber on a national forest for purposes of logging, or receipt of a grazing permit, are privileges obtained only for a consideration, much as in the case of private lands and other private property resources (though often, especially in the past, for less than their market value).[3]

Under the law (Mining Act of 1872), however, the public lands, with the exception of "primary-use" reservations such as parks and

[2] The original analyses of the allocation of common property resources (of a fishery) are by Gordon (12) and Scott (41). More recently the analysis has been extended by Smith (42) and others. For an informative review, see Haveman (15). The major finding of these studies is essentially that open access leads to overuse of the common property resource. As this is by now well understood we shall not dwell on it, rather concentrating on other aspects of public land management, including the conflicts that may arise between competing common property uses such as certain kinds of mining and recreation activities.

[3] By the same token, it should be noted that private property has at certain times and places been open access, or overexploited, or both. In this paper, however, we are concerned with management of the *public* lands and how this is appropriately affected by the presence of common property resources.

wilderness areas, are open to the public for exploration of certain types of minerals (the "hardrock" minerals). The availability of the public lands for mineral exploration represents a "common property" attribute. If the exploration is successful enough for a valid "patented" claim to be established, the title to the minerals and to all resources on the land overlying the claim is transferred in fee simple to the private party holding the patent. By this means public lands have under the mineral acts been transferred to private ownership, not unlike the transfer of ownership under the operation of the Homestead Act and other means of public lands alienation.

There are certain other common property attributes of resources that occur on public lands. Somewhat similar to the marine fisheries, which are the primary example of common property resources, fish and wildlife in the United States are publicly owned. They were originally viewed as common property in the common law. However, as early as the colonial period of American history responsibility for the regulation of game cropping tended to belong to the colonies. The migratory species, covered under international treaty, were exceptions, however. But the ownership by the individual states tends to be regarded as a stewardship of the wildlife held in trust for the people. In this sense, wildlife tends to be a common property resource subject to the right of capture under terms and conditions, albeit not usually involving a consideration, specified by the state. *Access* to the game across public land, moreover, is open, and accordingly use of the habitat occurring on federal lands for search and pursuit of wildlife, otherwise regulated, represents a common property feature of the public lands. This is a condition that most frequently does not obtain in connection with private lands.

Do other recreational resources partake of common property attributes? That is, are the resources giving rise to various types of environmental amenity services on public lands common property resources? The answer would seem to be yes, at least in part. To the extent that sunlight and air and meteorological phenomena are part of the recreational experience, we do have open access or common property resources associated with recreational use of public lands. But these common property features are not exclusively associated with public ownership. They are found similarly in association with private land—indeed, this is equally true of the distribution of fish and wildlife. And, access to recreation areas on public lands *is* subject to user charges (though often nominal, as in the case of admission fees to the national parks) and indeed, to exclusion, as when a campground is closed to further use.

In some instances, however, the administration of admissions reflects an open-access character. For example, charges are not typically made, nor fees collected, from visitors to the wilderness areas in the national forests. The reason for this, it would appear, is not necessarily that exclusion is impossible, but rather is in part the presumption that the capacity of these facilities is (has been) large in relation to the demand, and that efficient use requires a zero admission fee until such time as capacity limitations justify price rationing.

Beyond this, a preserved natural environment may be regarded as an open access resource for all who benefit from its existence without necessarily appearing on site to claim their rights or benefits. In this category are

1. vicarious consumers—those who derive satisfaction simply from knowing that certain rare or remarkable species and environments still exist, and indeed are willing to pay something for their "consumption," as evidenced by contributions to organizations such as the World Wildlife Fund or Nature Conservancy;
2. option demanders—those who value the option of experiencing a particular environment sometime in the future, perhaps for their children and grandchildren if not for themselves; and
3. those who may benefit from advances in such areas as medicine and agriculture, made possible by the preservation of genetic information in the more numerous wild species.

Of course, not all of these intangible benefits will be significant in any given natural area, but then neither will mineral deposits or merchantable timber.[4]

To summarize, we can say that the way a publicly owned natural asset is managed depends on how the rights to use its services are assigned. At one pole, the asset may be managed as a private property resource, with access limited by rights that are bought and sold, for example, logging rights. At the other, it may be managed as a common property resource, with open access, for example, hardrock mineral exploration, some wilderness recreation, and, of course, the "nonuser" uses listed above. There is also the possibility of some intermediate

---

[4] For a fuller discussion of the various types of nonuser benefits that may be provided by a preserved natural environment, see Krutilla (20), and Cicchetti and Fisher (5).

solution involving mixed, or partly private, management of the asset, for example, private riparian rights on a publicly owned natural asset. The definition of use or access rights is in turn determined by certain attributes of the asset, or perhaps in some cases just tradition, embodied in law and institution. The attributes that are particularly important in this connection, at least for the various amenity services, include non-excludability, absence of congestion, and something that might be termed *renewability* (i.e., the asset "recovers" so that use by one individual does not impair the asset for use by others). As these are variously taken to be defining characteristics of what are known as *public goods* (following Samuelson [39]), it is appropriate to look more closely at the relationship between the public lands, common property, and public goods.

PUBLIC LANDS, AND PUBLIC AND PRIVATE GOODS

A public good, as Samuelson defined it, is one whose consumption by one individual does not reduce its amount or availability for any other individual within the relevant set. In symbols, a pure public good is one for which the total output $X = X_A = X_B = \ldots, X_i$, where X_i equals the amount of the good going to individual i. The classical example is national defense. Police protection serves almost as well; and street lighting and flood hazard reduction provided through storage reservoirs are readily seen to meet this definition. The receipt of protection by one occupant of a flood plain does not reduce the amount of similar protection resulting from the flood stage reduction enjoyed by his neighbor. There naturally are public bads as well as goods; air and water pollution, landscape disfigurement, or general environmental degradation are examples. One person's smelling a pulp mill's fumes does not prevent another person's smelling them. Conversely, the elimination or prevention of a public bad is a public good. How do these considerations relate to the question of public lands and common property? We shall get to this presently, but first we need to investigate further some characteristics and qualifications attaching to public goods.

Although the Samuelsonian definition of the public good (bad) opens a way to investigate a previously neglected area, it was in retrospect discovered to be somewhat simplistic. Margolis (24), Davis and Whinston (8), and Mishan (28), among others, saw that the characteristic, consumption of a service by one does not reduce the quantity available to another, did not hold in general for many publicly provided services such as public education (especially when facilities are inadequate), service from insufficiently staffed police forces and crowded court calendars, and highways. In these cases we have what might be characterized as partly public goods, for which individual consumption $X_A = aX$, $0 \leqq a \leqq 1$, $X_B = bX$, $0 \leqq b \leqq 1$, ... In the special case of the pure public good defined above, the fraction a of total output X going to individual A, the fraction b of total output X going to individual B, and so on, are all equal to unity.

Similarly, they noted that the condition of "publicness" (if a good were available to one individual, it was indivisibly available to all) was not necessarily a technical condition of supply making it difficult or impossible to exclude any individual if it were made available to any other. While it may not be feasible to exclude a flood plain occupant from flood hazard reduction due to a storage facility upstream, it is physically possible to exclude a student from a school, a motorist from a freeway, or a recreationist from a wilderness, even if these facilities were provided or made available for use of another.

Finally, they recognized that even though a facility were privately provided, for example, a television antenna atop an apartment building (26), efficient allocation might require that other parties have free connections, since no additional cost would be attributable to the additional connections. This rule of course also applies to private theaters, stadia, and similar facilities that may have excess capacity, wherein the amount of the services received by one will not reduce the amount available to another.[5]

Accordingly, we have noted some difficulties with the original definition of public goods that have the following nature:

1. Conventional public services may be provided under conditions in which one person's availing himself of the service will diminish the amount available to another.
2. Conventional private services may be provided under conditions in which one person's availing himself of the service will *not* diminish the amount available to another.
3. Both public and private services may be provided under conditions

[5] For this to hold strictly, the seats would have to be subject to random selection rather than on a first-come, first-served basis, as the quality (quantity?) of the service for spectator events may be a function of the seat location of the observer, of the other observers, and of their number.

that may or may not be subject to exclusion, depending not only on *technical conditions* of production and consumption, but also on the assignments of ownership rights in law.

What then is the relationship between public goods and public lands and common property resources? First, it may be desirable, following Mishan (28, pp. 10 ff.), to avoid characterization of goods as public or private in light of the inescapable confusion with lay terminology and understanding involving public services. It is, for example, quite possible to develop a theory of public budgeting and expenditures without relying on the notion of *public goods* as discussed in the theoretical literature.[6] When we look at goods and services liberated from the need to consider their degree of "publicness," the indicated analysis can be performed with conventional concepts of market allocation criteria supplemented by the necessary adjustments found in the literature on externalities; this literature, in fact, justifies making provision for collective wants due to market failure. Market failure can result from the technical inability to exclude access to use of a jointly supplied service, which is incidental to, and simultaneous with, the production of a jointly produced bad. One can even make the case that each of the conditions mentioned above gives rise to goods, not only of varying degrees of "publicness," but also changing between their public and private character as capacity constraints (a) become effective with sufficient growth in demand and (b) are relaxed as additional investment is made in capacity to relieve excess demand—where the facilities *are not irreproducible assets.*

Given these relationships, there is no purpose in attempting to detail a relationship between public lands and public goods. There is no *necessary* relationship, and certainly no simple, straightforward one. Relationships arise more naturally between public lands and common property resources, as suggested in the preceding section, and between common property resources and public goods, the public good being the service provided by the former under conditions of no exclusion and of demand insufficient to generate congestion or marginal resource costs. Examples of this are wilderness recreation, up to a point, and the nonuser activities. What might be said more properly in connection with public lands and public goods is that we have here both private

---

[6] If not a theory of public expenditure, an adequate rationale for public intervention is presented in Bator (3), in Krutilla and Eckstein (21), and in Musgrave (31).

and collective consumption services of both private and common property resources, in numerous mixes and blends. Indeed, it is on the public lands that we can find almost every example of property right, class of good, and type of market failure. These, however, may all be discussed as particular types of externalities or indivisibilities on either the factor service or product side; a number of examples follow.

PUBLIC LANDS, AND OWNERSHIP AND
OTHER EXTERNALITIES

The residual public domain, the national forests, parks, wildlife refuges, and research natural areas, along with some special classes of land, are managed as public properties by the major land management agencies. Timbered and watered lands of the national forests and portions of the public domain offer perhaps the widest ranges of joint products or jointly supplied services. Because of the variety of resource interrelationships, numerous services are jointly supplied in varying proportions (unlike the classical case of "beef and hides"). The scenery within a tract of wildlands, for example, may represent on the one hand an example of a common property resource, a source of a private ownership externality as seen from a vantage point outside the boundary of the tract, and on the other a good without attributable resource costs, as viewed from within. In the first instance, access to the tract can be denied, yet the grosser visual attributes of the landscape can, in many instances, be viewed from without the boundaries, and this represents a limitation on the power of the management agency to regulate access (and therefore extract payment for the benefits) through the extent of its ownership. In the second instance, while access to forest land may be controlled, viewing the landscape from within the boundaries of a national forest does not incur, to a point, either resource or congestion costs attributable to the viewer. If the scenery, moreover, is jointly supplied with campsites essential to its viewing, but these are primitive, undeveloped sites not involving resource costs (including damage to the ecological environment to an appreciable extent), there would be no warrant to exclude visitation on nonpayment of a fee, as there would be no costs associated with the viewing. To this point all the services of the landscape, both visual attributes and congenial undeveloped sites on which to make camp, should be supplied without marginal user charges, since no resource

44

costs have been incurred.[7] If the "open-access" policy coupled with the demand for the services of this area result in reaching a capacity restriction, charges then could be employed to ration capacity when it is exceeded by demand. This is, of course, the classic common property management problem referred to in note 2. Note, however, that the capacity limitation relates to only one of the jointly supplied, complementary, services—the campsites. Access to them is subject to regulation or exclusion *as a matter of policy, it being otherwise technically feasible to do so.* Some attributes of the landscape are jointly consumed (scenery and campsites used in reaching a vantage point for viewing), where one is technically not subject to exclusion (visual stimuli) or diminution by use; and consumption of the other, though subject to exclusion, also has no attributable costs until a point is reached where congestion sets in.

This illustration presents an example of jointly supplied services which provide positive utility to the consumers. There is, of course, a somewhat different case where joint production results in a positive good and a negative good, or bad, which inflicts uncompensated costs on others who would use the services of the environment with none of its attributes impaired.

Before proceeding with some examples, it might be helpful to define precisely what is meant by *externality* and how it is distinguished from the related concepts of *jointness in supply* and Samuelsonian *publicness.* Accordingly, an externality is said to exist "whenever an output of one economic agent appears as an input in the consumption or production vector of another," without accompanying payment (18, p. 79). This can be represented symbolically as $A = (X_{1A}, -X_{1A}{}^E, X_{2A})$; $B = (X_{1B}, X_{1A \cdot B}{}^E, X_{2B})$, where A and B are activity vectors (consumption or production) of agents (consumers or firms) A and B respectively, X_{ij} is the input of good i to agent j, $i = 1, 2$, $j = A, B$, $-X_{1A}{}^E$ is an (unpriced) output associated with A's use of 1, and $X_{1A \cdot B}{}^E$ is an (unpriced) input to B from A's use of 1.[8] The externality is $X_{1A \cdot B}{}^E$ in this framework, which is easily extended from the two goods–two persons case represented here for simplicity.

[7] There *is* a case for lump-sum payment to capture the (external) site rent. We shall abstract for the moment from the case where returns from exploitation of associated resources are precluded by retention of the area in its natural state. This relates to evaluation for a specific allocation decision, as contrasted with admissions policy after the allocation decision has been made.

[8] Our notation here is adopted from Holtermann (19), and is also consistent with Meade (25), and Buchanan and Stubblebine (4), the classic references.

Now suppose there is a third agent, C, who also receives an (un-priced) input $X_{1A \cdot C}{}^E$ from A's use of 1. If the externality is a public good, then $-X_{1A}{}^E = X_{1A \cdot B}{}^E = X_{1A \cdot C}{}^E$, from the definition of a public good given earlier.

Jointness in supply of what has been called a mixed good (6) can also be represented in this framework. A mixed good is one, like a scenic natural area, having both a public component (the scenery) and a private one (the campsites). If we designate this good as X_3, then consumption of its public aspect, X_3, is $X_3' = X_{3A}' = X_{3B}' = X_{3C}' = \ldots$, and of its private, X_3'', is $X_3'' = X_{3A}'' + X_{3B}'' + X_{3C}'' + \ldots$.

Now let us imagine a setting similar to our previous example in which people visit an area in order to enjoy the scenery, remoteness from industrial-urban activity, and solitude. Imagine further the discovery of mineral deposits leading to establishment of a valid mineral claim on this setting followed by patent. The working of the deposit, assume, requires the removal of substantial overburden and related landscape modification for ore beneficiation, tailing ponds, and related facilities, significant in relation to the total scenic area. Recall that in the first example the use of the area by any viewer did not reduce the aesthetic stimuli that were available to any other. Moreover, to the extent that any costs imposed by the viewers arose as the result of congestion, it was *reciprocal without* real income or utility *redistribution*.[9]

The nature of the externalities occasioned by the mining in the second illustration, however, is different in that there is a *unidirectional* rather than a reciprocal relationship between competing uses of the visual environment, *with attendant utility redistributive effects*.[10] Rothenberg (37) has used these distinctions to characterize the essential difference between *congestion*—namely, the identical use of the environment by all parties who suffer reciprocally inflicted costs, but not, within limits, damages to the environment (Rothenberg's constructive use of the environment)—and *pollution*—namely, a competing dissimilar use of the environment which alters the characteristics of the environmental resources in a way that is in some sense destructive, and in which there is a unidirectional flow of the costs associated with resource exploita-

---

[9] This is a little too strong. The negative externality need not be equally valued by all those who impose it on each other.

[10] Mining is taken only as an example of a class of uses covered by developmental or extractive activities such as road building and logging in roadless de facto wilderness, and construction of roads along or dams across wild rivers, where physical aspects of natural environments are irreversibly altered.

tion.[11] In the context of a discussion of common property resources, the situation described above might be characterized as one of between-group as well as within-group competition for a resource by two (or more) different common property uses.

If we accept, at least tentatively, the Rothenberg distinctions, (with some support from Mishan [28]) we now come to what is a very significant aspect relating to the matter of evaluating the relative worth of alternative incompatible uses to which given natural areas, or public wild lands, may be put. In confronting the choice between incompatible alternative uses of natural environments, as will be the case in allocating de facto wilderness and wild and scenic rivers under the current legislation[12] (and in considering management of these and other multiple-use areas), the redistributive aspects enter directly into the evaluation of opportunity costs of alternative incompatible uses.

The problem here is an old one in welfare economics: how to properly evaluate a project or land use policy which results in gains to some individuals and losses to others. In particular, can the gains and losses be algebraically added over all affected individuals to determine the net gain (from each of the alternative uses of an area's resources)? Underlying any policy prescription from a benefit-cost analysis of a resource use project is the potential Pareto, or Kaldor (19)- Hicks (17), criterion; according to this criterion the project is efficient, and presumably therefore desirable, if the gains exceed the losses, so that the gainers can in principle compensate the losers and have a positive residual gain. This was amended by Scitovsky (40), who proposed that no unambiguous improvement in welfare is associated with undertaking a project that is efficient in the sense of Kaldor and Hicks unless, at the same time, it is possible to show that the prospective losers could not bribe the prospective gainers to forego the project,

[11] Nelson (32) commenting on the Rothenberg characterization observed a qualification in connection with, at least, use of automobiles in which there may be not only the reciprocal externalities of congestion, but also an environmentally destructive air quality deterioration. In some cases, where there are multiple-source noxious effluents of a mobile character, there will be competition for the resource (clean air, a common property resource technically given) as well as for use of the travel route (technically a private property resource, used under open-access conditions given by law or policy). In this instance the Rothenberg characterization reflects characteristics of both cases discussed here. Unless unregulated use of trails and campsites have an ecologically damaging effect on the environment, the Nelson criticism would not apply to the examples presented here.

[12] This is a task implicit in the Wilderness Act of 1964, the Wild and Scenic Rivers Act of 1968, and the National Environmental Policy Act of 1969.

or return to the status quo ante. Of course, even this is not satisfactory to one who is concerned about the actual distribution of gains and losses from alternative uses of an environment (or any other resource endowment).[13] Perhaps the only sensible way to proceed here is to follow Harberger (14), who argues that the simple aggregation underlying estimation of net benefits and costs of a project or policy is simply the best we can hope for in applied welfare analysis, and that this information ought to be one component, but not necessarily the only one, in a decision as to its desirability.

Measurement of the gains and losses associated with a change in the allocation of resources, however, is not entirely a straightforward exercise, even conceptually, when rights to use the resources at issue are often ambiguously defined. How can this be when the by-now well-known Coase (7) theorem states that resource allocation, explicitly, and resource valuation, implicitly, are invariant with respect to the assignment of property rights? Taking the explicit part of the theorem first, it states that a resource, such as a piece of land, subject to competing uses will be put to its optimal, or highest valued use, regardless of the initial assignment of the rights to it. In the example given above, if the site in question is worth more to a wealthy environmentalist, say, then to the holder of a patented mining claim, the environmentalist simply buys out the miner, and the site is left undisturbed. If it is worth more to the miner, he refuses the bid, and develops the site for minerals production. The analysis is symmetric if rights to use of the site initially lie with the environmentalist, only now the roles are reversed. The environmentalist refuses the miner's offer if the site is worth more to him undisturbed, and accepts it, and the resulting landscape disfigurement, otherwise. In each case, the land and related resources are put to their highest valued use, which is clearly the same regardless of who has to compensate whom. Implicit in the theorem is the presumption that evaluations of the alternatives are not affected by the prior distribution of property rights. In our example the land is worth a certain amount to the environmentalist, which amount he is willing to pay in the event that the miner has title, and will accept in the event that the land is his to dispose of.

If the explicit and implicit statements of the Coase theorem are valid, then it seems that contrary to the assertion made at the start

[13] For a careful and rigorous, though not very helpful, discussion of this point, in the larger context of evaluating changes in real national income, see Samuelson (38).

of the preceding paragraph, measurement of the gains and losses from a project is in fact straightforward and unambiguous. There are, however, a couple of problems—not with the logic of the theorem, but with its application in typical environmental externality situations, as pointed out perhaps most clearly by Mishan (27)—which further consideration of our example can bring out.

Recall that on one side of the bargaining table is a wealthy environmentalist. Now, if instead of this single individual there were a great many, thousands, or even millions of consumers who would suffer in one way or another a welfare loss from conversion of a particular scenic natural area into a mining operation, it could be very costly to evaluate and represent the interest of each. The costs of negotiation, or more generally, the transaction costs, in this situation could be so high that even though the value to all consumers of the site's amenity services together exceeds the value to the mining firm, assignment of property rights to the firm, as under current mining law, would result in use of the site for mining.

A second problem with application of the theorem, and one that bears directly on the evaluations of alternatives under differing property regimes, is indicated by the assumption that the environmentalist is "wealthy." The problem is very simply that the amount a consumer would be willing to pay for a given resource configuration will in general be less than the amount he would accept to depart from it, owing to the income constraint in the former case. Perhaps a better illustration of the significance of this point is the selective process in kidnapping. Wealthy families and corporations are the universal victims, presumably because of their greater ability to pay large ransoms, and not because poor folks are less attached to (willing to accept less for) their offspring. Although this is admittedly an extreme case, it emphasizes the potential range of values given by measures of consumer's surplus that are respectively constrained and unconstrained by income. Similarly, many people who are not particularly wealthy feel that only with reluctance would they accept the loss of a natural area important to them or as part of a national heritage to their children and grandchildren. This is not to suggest that the implied reservation prices would be easy to determine (any more than would the amounts people would be "willing to pay" under an alternative property regime) or even that this is necessarily the appropriate regime. Again, the point is simply that valuation of a common property environmental resource is, as suggested, not entirely straightforward.

49

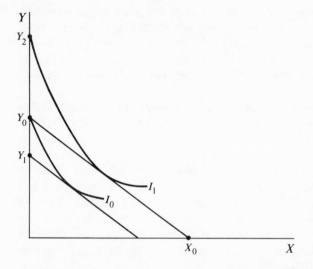

Figure 1

The variation in value corresponding in general to different assignments of property rights can be demonstrated with the aid of a diagram. In figure 1, Y represents the (aggregate) market good, let us say the output of the mine, and X the environmental amenity. If the miner has the initial property right, then the consumer with budget line $Y_0 X_0$ would be willing to pay an amount (compensating variation) equal to $Y_0 - Y_1$, which would leave him just as well off as before the transaction (on his original indifference curve I_0) for the right to use (part of) the site for its amenity services.[14] Note that he could not in any case pay more than Y_0; his willingness to pay is bounded by his income.

Now suppose property rights to the environment are vested in the consumer. Again assuming his consumption opportunities are described by line $Y_0 X_0$, the amount he would accept in return for his right to consume X is given by the intersection of indifference curve I_1 with with the Y axis, Y_2 in the diagram. By keeping him on the same indifference curve we again insure that he is just as well off after the transaction as before, but note that this requires following the curve I_1 until it reaches the Y axis—independently of initial income Y_0. Clearly, $Y_2 - Y_0$ can, and in the typical case will, exceed $Y_0 - Y_1$.[15]

[14] See Mishan (27) for a detailed discussion of the compensating and equivalent variation concepts of consumer's surplus, and the sufficiency of the former for our purposes.

[15] This follows from the assumption that the income, or welfare, effect is positive. See Mishan (27, p. 127).

In order to determine whether the net benefit from, say, preservation of the environmental resource is positive, it is necessary to take the difference between the aggregate over all consumer-environmentalists of one or the other of the compensating variation consumer's surplus measures described above and the value of the resource to the mining firm. Note that where the competing use is by a profit-maximizing producer of an intermediate good traded on a competitive market and with access to capital markets, as is presumably the case for the mining firm, the two measures collapse to a single figure, the excess revenue from use of the site in question, which gives its value to the firm. In defense of Coase, his examples are primarily producer-to-producer externalities, so that neither transaction costs nor the ambiguity produced by consumer income effects legitimately influence his results. It is our view, however, that the typical externality situation arising out of competing claims to the use of environmental resources on the public lands is better represented in our example, in which both effects are likely to be significant.[16]

If it is accepted that there are in theory two (potentially significantly different) measures of the value of any environmental amenity services provided by a tract of public land, the question naturally arises, Which is appropriate? Or can the difference perhaps be resolved? Consideration of the unique valuation by the mining firm suggests an appealing market solution to the latter question. Suppose a private firm is given the right, perhaps as a result of a competitive bid, to sell the wilderness camping and related recreational services of the tract of land. Then we are back in a Coasian world of (at most) two-party negotiation, based on unique valuation of each of the alternatives by private profit-maximizing producers with access to capital markets (and a determinate optimal solution).

This idea might well be tried, at least on an experimental basis, but we foresee at least a couple of difficulties. First, the land in part may necessarily be common property, or open access, due to the public good nature of some of the services it provides—the nonuser uses touched upon in our earlier discussion of common property resources. In other words, as suggested in the introduction, although a market solution

[16] It may not be too much to suggest that one's position on the "Coase controversy" is determined by one's model of externality. If so, this would be a good example of Milton Friedman's proposition that differences in positions taken by economists on various issues result not so much from differences in theory as from differences in (sometimes implicit) empirical judgments, which may, however, be resolved by further empirical work.

could uniquely determine value, the resulting allocation would probably not be optimal due to the lack of incentive to take account of all the benefits of nonextractive use or, for that matter, all the costs of extractive use, including too-rapid exploitation due to a private discount rate above the social rate.[17] Second, a market solution may be politically infeasible since many outdoor recreationists appear to regard "free" access to wilderness on the public lands as a part of their inalienable heritage.[18]

In the event that market resolution of the difference is not feasible, then which measure is appropriate? The answer to this question is neither obvious nor entirely satisfactory. What is at issue is use of common property resources. In theory, all should enjoy equal access to their benefits. While an open pit mine will reduce the benefits of the scenic and related aesthetic attributes of the landscape for some, thereby effectively restricting their rights to enjoy an undisturbed natural environment, the denial of the mining rights is also a restriction on the rights of the mining enterprise. The same observation, of course, is applicable to the logging of a tract of land which results in landscape degradation or in altering the characteristics of a scenic or wild river. The question is, Who should have to buy out whom? Who has the original rights? If the position of "ethical neutrality," advanced by Coase (7) and further elaborated by Demsetz (9, 10), is accepted, then those who would seek to infringe the rights of the mining enterprise, for example, would have an obligation to compensate that enterprise for its losses from denial of mining access as readily justified as would the mining enterprise to compensate the losers from the landscape disfigurement. Indeed, the strict Coasian would presumably reject the notion of unidirectional externality and the Rothenberg distinctions based upon it.

A variation of the no-prior-assignment of rights, or the case of ethical neutrality, has recently been advanced by Mohring and Boyd (30). All open-access rights are required to be withdrawn, in this case,

---

[17] Although the discussion here is in the context of *static* externality, the really interesting problems of market failure on the public lands arise in a dynamic setting, as the mention of option value (earlier) and discounting would suggest. These problems are treated at length elsewhere, for example in Krutilla (20), Fisher, Krutilla, and Cicchetti (11), and especially in the longer volume cited in the footnote identifying the authors.

[18] This attitude filters through responses of wilderness recreationists to survey questions about their values and preferences in regard to wilderness management. See Hammack and Brown (13).

and all formerly common property resources are to be converted to private property resources. Access to any resource under this doctrine would involve allocation to the highest bid, whether by prospective final- or intermediate-service users. Here the willingness-to-pay criterion, based on the measure of consumer surplus bounded by relevant income constraints, would be the indicated criterion of value. All parties have equal access in return for a consideration, as all are excluded in the absence of payments to the agency managing a restricted-access resource. Alternatively, symmetry could be preserved by giving rights to all and requiring compensation for any infringement.

Another method of assignment of rights has been that of prior appropriation, or prior use. This is the basic legal doctrine, with numerous variations, attaching to the allocation of water rights in western regions of the United States, and is basically the method of assigning rights among different contenders for mineral rights on public lands. Also, it might be noted, it seems to be consistent with a pure Pareto criterion in that it implicitly requires anyone wanting a change from the status quo to *actually* compensate those who would lose thereby (the "squatters"). While the establishment of valid claims to mineral resources has not been without its ambiguities in western history, these appear to be trival compared with determining the priority of use between recreationists and prospectors in today's controversies over use of public lands. This problem may well be of a lesser order of magnitude in connection with new sources of pollution in the urban-industrial environment, but seems to afford little prospect of ready resolution for problems arising in the context of public land use.

An alternative water rights doctrine relates to the accessibility of water to riparian owners, to the extent that the uses do not diminish the supply in quantity or quality. While the use of water under the riparian doctrine has not observed the provision of water quality maintenance in practice, it introduces the elements of the rights to the usufruct of common property resources. Consumer sovereignty is partially constrained; property rights are vested in private parties only in part. Here the services can be utilized, provided that the substance of the resource is left intact. This doctrine provides a link to the Rothenberg distinction between the "constructive" and "destructive" uses of the environment.

It is obvious that pursuing this question much further would lead us out of economics and into ethics. There are deep philosophical issues here, which have been raised also by conservationists and environmentalists, and on which we do not feel particularly qualified to pronounce.[19] Nevertheless, as they have been raised, and are so interesting, we will offer just a few observations. An argument has been advanced by Page (34) for justifying a hierarchy of rights based on the difference between rights to use of the services of a common property resource, which does not impair the substance, and rights to consumption, preemption, or destruction of the resource itself. Is there a basis for making a valid ethical distinction? It appears that an argument of some persuasiveness can be advanced, depending on the nature of the destructive use—namely, the severity of its detrimental effect, and duration, for human welfare.

The gravity of the threat to human welfare stemming from a destructive use of the environment may well evoke a valid moral judgment. Where health and life itself is jeopardized by pollution, the law is quite clear. The law regarding emission of noxious substances into air and water, media on which the community's most basic elements of welfare depend, is a clear assignment of priority, to which matters of "willingness to pay" are regarded as irrelevant.[20] But where the infringement of rights to the usufruct of common property resources involves only matters of convenience or a consideration of aesthetics, the courts have not yet rendered a conclusive judgment.

The matter of the duration of damages, or rights infringement, has drawn attention in the debate over the responsibility for compensation. This essentially dynamic problem of long-run resource use is addressed in detail elsewhere (11, 2), but a few remarks can be ventured. If a destructive use of environmental resources involves a welfare loss in perpetuity, irrespective of its implications for the more basic constituents of human welfare, a case has been made (28) for giving different weights or priority to the rights based on the constructive-destructive distinction made in the use of the environment. The studies referred to here arrive at essentially the same result (abstracting from the matter of severity of damage) though they start implicitly with the more conservative Mohring-Boyd symmetry assumption. That is to say, when a destructive use of common property resources has an irreversible effect or is remediable only at great cost and difficulty,

[19] These are basically issues involving the ethical base of the doctrine of consumer sovereignty. See Rawls (36) for discussion in a much more general context, and Leopold (23) for an application of ethical arguments specifically to problems of land and other environmental resource use.

[20] See, for example, the Clean Air Act of 1967.

there is some value to keeping the option that would be foreclosed by the destructive alternative. This is particularly true if it is not certain what the demand is for the services of either of the alternative uses, and if information about demand, or anticipated benefits, results in the revision of anticipations and plans. Note that while this does not have implications for the assignment of priority of access rights, the direction of the influence on the allocation of uses is the same as in the case where liability for compensation devolves upon the proposed destructive use.

To summarize the discussion of this section, in marginal cases a difference in outcomes may be caused by the assumption as to who is liable for the opportunity returns foreclosed by the preclusion of one of two (or more) incompatible alternative allocations of common property resources. The willingness to pay on the part of nondestructive uses represents the lower bound value of the resource when allocated to such a purpose. It is, moreover, based on a polar interpretation of the priority in a possible hierarchy of rights. If the destructive use is one sufficiently grave to elicit valid moral judgments, the correct measure of the destroyed usufruct may require priority in the consideration of rights, with the responsibility for compensation on the destructive use. Compensation in such cases may well be substantially greater than the sum which the losers would be willing (or able) to pay to avoid the losses. If the question is one of health, life, or survival of the species, then absolute prohibition, the practical equivalent of infinite compensation, may be justified; this has been the case, as a matter of law and policy, in recognition of the irrelevance of market-determined distribution of income. Finally, when there occurs a destructive use of the environment, one having a nonzero probability of an irreversible adverse consequence, an additional value—namely, that of retaining options open—must also be weighed in a final determination.

CONCLUSIONS

The major findings of this paper can be summarized as follows:

1. There is a very large residual public domain in the United States. However, the distribution of resources on it is somewhat different from that on already alienated lands—more heavily weighted on the

55

side of environmental amenities, less on the side of commercially developable resources.

2. For many though not all uses, the public lands are managed as common property resources, for both technical and institutional reasons. Although management of common property resources is now fairly well understood, at least in theory, more difficult issues arise on the public lands as a result of competing claims of dissimilar common property uses, such as mining and recreation.

3. Where values of these competing uses must be weighed, as in a benefit-cost analysis for a public decision on allocation, a problem arises. The value of the resource in an important class of uses—namely, those like recreation in which the resource service enters directly the utility functions of consumers—is not uniquely determined. Rather, contrary to the Coasian presumption, it will vary with the assignment of property rights. Where a competing use (say, mining) has the initial rights, value to the recreationist is determined by his income-constrained maximum willingness-to-pay to buy out the miner. Where the recreationist has the initial rights, value is determined by the unconstrained minimum amount he will accept in exchange for his rights. Since these two measures of value are in general not the same, assignment of property rights may determine the outcome, in marginal cases, of a decision to allocate a resource to its optimal, or highest-valued, use.

4. This suggests the question, Which measure is appropriate? Who should have the initial rights? The answer is not obvious, though a better case can perhaps be made for assigning priority to the nondestructive use rather than to the destructive one. A result that has similar allocative implications also emerges from analysis of the effect of irreversibility in an uncertain economic environment.

REFERENCES

1. Arrow, K. J. "The Organization of Economic Activity: Issues Pertinent to the Choice of Market versus Nonmarket Allocation," in *The Analysis and Evaluation of Public Expenditures: The PPB System* (Washington: Government Printing Office, 1969).
2. Arrow, K. J., and Fisher, A. C. "Environmental Preservation, Uncertainty, and Irreversibility," *Quarterly Journal of Economics,* in press.
3. Bator, F. M. "The Anatomy of Market Failure," *Quarterly Journal of Economics,* vol. 72, no. 3 (August 1958).

4. Buchanan, J. M., and Stubblebine, W. C. "Externality," *Economica*, N. S., vol. 29 (1962).
5. Cicchetti, C. J., and Fisher, A. C. "Economic Values on Environmental Resources: Some Observations on the Supreme Court Decision in the Mineral King Case." Mimeographed. 1972.
6. Cicchetti, C. J., and Smith, V. K. "A Note on Jointly Supplied Mixed Goods," *Quarterly Review of Economics and Business*, vol. 10, no. 3 (August 1970).
7. Coase, R. H. "The Problem of Social Cost," *Journal of Law and Economics*, vol. 3 (October 1960).
8. Davis, O. A., and Whinston, A. B. "On the Distinction Between Public and Private Goods," *American Economic Review*, vol. 57, no. 2 (May 1967).
9. Demsetz, H. "The Exchange and Enforcement of Property Rights," *Journal of Law and Economics*, vol. 7 (October 1964).
10. ————. "Some Aspects of Property Rights," *Journal of Law and Economics*, vol. 9 (October 1966).
11. Fisher, A. C., Krutilla, J. V., and Cicchetti, C. J. "The Economics of Environmental Preservation," *American Economic Review*, vol. 62 (September 1972).
12. Gordon, H. S. "The Economic Theory of a Common Property Resource: The Fishery," *Journal of Political Economy*, vol. 62 (April 1954).
13. Hammack, J., and Brown, G. M. *Waterfowl and Wetlands: Toward Bioeconomic Analysis*. Baltimore: The Johns Hopkins University Press for Resources for the Future, Inc., 1974.
14. Harberger, A. C. "Three Basic Postulates for Applied Welfare Economics: An Interpretive Essay," *Journal of Economic Literature*, vol. 9 (September 1971).
15. Haveman, R. H. "Common Property, Congestion, and Environmental Pollution," *Quarterly Journal of Economics*, vol. 87 (May 1973).
16. Head, J. G. "Public Goods and Public Policy," *Public Finance*, vol. 17, no. 3 (1962).
17. Hicks, J. R. "Foundations of Welfare Economics," *Economic Journal*, vol. 49 (1939).
18. Holtermann, S. E. "Externalities and Public Goods," *Economica*, N. S., vol. 39 (February 1972).
19. Kaldor, N. "Welfare Propositions of Economics and Interpersonal Comparisons of Utility," *Economic Journal*, vol. 49 (1939).
20. Krutilla, J. V. "Conservation Reconsidered," *American Economic Review*, vol. 57 (September 1967).
21. Krutilla, J. V., and Eckstein, O. *Multiple Purpose River Development: Studies in Applied Economic Analysis*. Baltimore: The Johns Hopkins Press for Resources for the Future, Inc., 1958.

22. Leibenstein, H. "The Proportionality Controversy and the Theory of Production," *Quarterly Journal of Economics,* vol. 69 (November 1955).
23. Leopold, A. *A Sand County Almanac.* London: Oxford University Press, 1949.
24. Margolis, J. "A Comment on the Pure Theory of Public Expenditure," *Review of Economics and Statistics,* vol. 37, no. 4 (November 1955).
25. Meade, J. E. "External Economies and Diseconomies in a Competitive Situation," *Economic Journal,* vol. 62 (1952).
26. Minasian, J. R. "Television Pricing and the Theory of Public Goods," *Journal of Law and Economics,* vol. 7 (October 1964).
27. Mishan, E. J. *Cost-Benefit Analysis.* New York: Praeger Publishers, 1971.
28. ———. "The Postwar Literature on Externalities: An Interpretive Essay," *Journal of Economic Literature,* vol. 9, no. 1 (March 1971).
29. ———. "The Relationship Between Joint Products, Collective Goods, and External Effects," *Journal of Political Economy,* vol. 77, no. 3 (May/June 1969).
30. Mohring, H., and Boyd, J. H. "Analyzing Externalities: Direct Interaction vs. Asset Utilization Frameworks," *Economica,* N. S., vol. 38 (November 1971).
31. Musgrave, R. A. *Theory of Public Finance: A Study in Public Economy.* New York: McGraw-Hill Book Co., 1959.
32. Nelson, R. "Discussion," *American Economic Review,* vol. 60, no. 2 (May 1970).
33. Nickel, W. F., III. "The Current Legal Status of Ownership and Management of Fish and Wildlife on the Public Lands." Paper prepared as part of the Clinical Program in Environmental Law, The National Law Center, George Washington University, Washington, D.C., June 1971.
34. Page, T. *Economics of Involuntary Transfers.* New York: Springer Verlag, 1973.
35. Patinkin, D. "Demand Curves and Consumer's Surplus," in *Measurement in Economics: Studies in Mathematical Economics and Econometrics in Memory of Yehuda Grunfeld,* edited by Carl F. Christ and others. Stanford, Calif.: Stanford University Press, 1963.
36. Rawls, J. *A Theory of Justice.* Cambridge, Mass.: Harvard University Press, 1971.
37. Rothenberg, J. "The Economics of Congestion and Pollution: An Integrated View," *American Economic Review,* vol. 60, no. 2 (May 1970).
38. Samuelson, P. A. "Evaluation of Real National Income," *Oxford Economic Papers,* N. S., vol. 2 (1950).
39. ———. "The Pure Theory of Public Expenditure," *Review of Economics and Statistics,* vol. 36 (November 1954).

40. Scitovsky, T. S. "A Note on Welfare Propositions in Economics," *Review of Economic Studies,* vol. 9 (1941).
41. Scott, A. "The Fishery: The Objectives of Sole Ownership," *Journal of Political Economy,* vol. 63 (April 1955).
42. Smith, V. "Economics of Production from Natural Resources," *American Economic Review,* vol. 58 (June 1968).
43. Weisbrod, B. A. "Collective-Consumption Services of Individual-Consumption Goods," *Quarterly Journal of Economics,* vol. 78, no. 3 (August 1964).

MARION CLAWSON

Comment

THIS PAPER starts with the conventional distinction between common property resources, to which it is alleged that access is free, and private property, access to which is closed and which it is assumed the owner manages in his own long-term interest; it adds considerations of irreversibility, irreproductibility, and externalities; and concludes (in part) "when a destructive use of common property resources has an irreversible effect, or is remediable only at great cost and difficulty, there is some value to keeping open the option that would be foreclosed by the destructive alternative." I had intuitively arrived at this conclusion, and since it coincides with my biases, it is obviously sound. But I am disappointed at the process by which the authors arrive at this conclusion, for I think it does not recognize the complexities of the real world.

As a pragmatist concerned to conduct empirical research on problems apparent to me, I try to deal with the real world as I perceive it, of course. The complexities of that world make research difficult, and there is merit in abstraction; but there is also danger, in that readers, and perhaps the researcher himself, come to accept the abstraction as the reality. The situation as to land, even publicly owned land, is complex; and there is grave danger that a simplistic treatment of its use will be misleading.

Property owned in common, whether land or other kinds, has not by any means always been freely open to any user, nor is property owned in common today in many parts of the world open to any user. Social controls of many kinds have existed, and do exist, to limit and govern the use of property owned in common. Such social controls often regulate the intensity of use. Property owned in common has not invariably been used in an exploitative way; conversion of common

The author is Acting President, Resources for the Future, Inc.

property has not invariably led to conservative use—in fact, sometimes the opposite has occurred. Cropland in the United States, almost invariably privately owned, has been subjected to severe soil erosion, and it has been public efforts which helped to modify use of these private lands; publicly owned forests in the United States have been used with more care and more thought for the future than have privately owned forests; and publicly owned grazing lands in the United States today are used with as much care for preservation of their productive capacity as are privately owned grazing lands.

Wantrup has put it very well:

Common property of natural resources in itself is no more a tragedy in terms of environmental depletion than private property. It all depends on what social institutions—that is, decision systems on the second level—are guiding resource use in either case. Effective institutions to conserve common-property resources have been developed for the administration of public forests in many countries. The same is true for the conservation of game and fish whether by primitive tribes in pre-Columbian America or modern game management departments. Agricultural land held in common by villages in medieval Europe was conserved by institutions based on custom and law before private property and the profit motive broke up these decision systems.[1] During the colonial period of the 18th and 19th centuries the spread of private property rights in resources did not prevent serious depletion of forests, range, and agricultural land in many parts of the world.[2]

Privately owned property is not invariably closed to public access. By long custom and common law, hundreds or thousands of miles of footpaths on private land are open to public use in Great Britain today. By pressure of public opinion, without benefit of law, millions of acres of privately owned forests are freely open to public recreation use in the United States today. Most private property today may be used by the public only with the consent of the owner; but this is far from invariably true.

The authors recognize that federal lands have some attributes of private land, in that access is not invariably freely open to all comers. But federal lands often acquire entrenched private uses, which are or may be legally "privilege" as the Forest Service has always asserted grazing permits are, but which politically take on many characteristics of "rights." Even when the forms of impartial sale by competitive

[1] S. V. Ciriacy-Wantrup, "Social Conservation in European Farm Management," *Journal of Farm Economics*, vol. 20, no. 3 (February 1938), pp. 86–101.
[2] S. V. Ciriacy-Wantrup, "The Economics of Environmental Policy," *Land Economics*, vol. 47, no. 1 (February 1971), p. 43.

bidding are observed, the choice of the successful bidder is far from random—some parties are in vastly better position to acquire the use or the products of the federal land than are others.

Much of the public land of the United States was transferred to private ownership in literally millions of separate transactions. Prior to such transfer to private ownership, much of the public land was used by individuals without any effective controls on their use, and in the process many resources were used exploitatively, some to destruction —the passenger pigeon, for instance. But, even at the height of the public-private transfer process, the public lands were not equally open to all possible users; indeed, one of the persistent and merited criticisms of this transfer process was that the public lands were, in fact, and for various reasons, closed to large segments of the total public. Exploitative use of resources in the United States has never been confined to property held in common; it has been rampant on privately owned resources as well; and property owned in common has in some cases been used as conservatively as technical knowledge of the day indicated was necessary.

In the management of the federal lands, prices have played various roles; some products are sold at something approaching competitive prices while others are free or at legislatively established prices which bear little relation to present-day market prices. In the management of such lands, there is a trade-off between economic and administrative controls; that is, where prices are below market, because of legislative or administrative decision, administrative controls must take over much of the regulatory function that prices play in a private market.

The resource use picture of the world is infinitely more complex than a simple dichotomy between common property resources open to all users (and often assumed to be exploitatively used) and private property resources, used as the owner decides (and often assumed to include a careful balancing of present versus future production and income). Natural resources owned in common are used under a wide variety of arrangements, ranging from free access to highly controlled access, and ranging from use without any restraints to use under highly detailed restraints. Likewise, privately owned natural resources are used under a wide variety of arrangements, ranging from virtually no social controls to very strict ones. In the United States today, virtually no private property within or adjacent to urban areas may be used entirely on the basis of the owners' wishes; many kinds of social controls limit the use of such property. These social controls have

62

been established by various governmental processes; one may reasonably conclude that such controls largely if not fully reflect the convictions of the electorate in the relevant governmental unit. Social controls over the use of private property have been extended almost steadily over the past sixty to one hundred years; there is every reason to expect that they will continue to be extended, in forms not always evident now.

As one who has long been concerned with the management and use of public lands, I welcome the entry of other scholars into this subject matter. Their conclusion about preserving options for future use of property held in common seems to me to be equally valid for property privately owned. Does this mean that the conclusion does not naturally or invariably flow from the starting assumptions? I urge these researchers to continue their studies and to include a wider range of land use control mechanisms and arrangements in their future studies.

PAUL PORTNEY, JON SONSTELIE, & ALLEN KNEESE

Environmental quality, household migration, and collective choice

INTRODUCTION

THE NATURAL environment of a metropolitan region may be taken to consist of the surrounding air mantle, watercourses, large landscape features, climate and weather, soil conditions, and the associated biological systems. Human activities in such a region influence the quality of this natural environment in various ways—usually for the worse. But at a cost, often at a large cost, these adverse impacts can be controlled and managed so as to maintain environmental standards. In some instances, environmental circumstances can be improved; for example, artificial landscape features such as lakes may be created which are more attractive than the natural landscape.

The quality of the natural environment presents a special problem for resource allocation which market processes cannot resolve, at least not fully. This is because it is, to a greater or lesser extent, a public good. That is, environmental quality exhibits jointness in supply in the sense that large groups of residents of an airshed, for example, will experience roughly the same air quality. Furthermore, improvements in air quality cannot generally be achieved in such a way as to exclude certain residents in the same way that nonpurchasers can be denied the consumption of private goods.

There are two main contexts in which to view the production and consumption of such public goods. The first is one in which the con-

The authors are respectively a Senior Research Associate, Resources for the Future, Inc.; a Research Associate, Resources for the Future, Inc.; and Professor, Department of Economics, University of New Mexico. We wish to thank the Edna McConnell Clark Foundation for the financial assistance necessary to undertake this study. We wish also to thank Ed Haefele, whose ideas have prompted much of this research, as well as Cliff Russell, Mark Sharefkin, Martin McGuire, and John Ferejohn, who commented on an earlier version of this paper.

suming population is fixed, community boundaries are drawn, and the tax and regulation systems used to finance the public provision of public goods or to force their provision by private interests are also fixed. (Private provision is important because improved air and water quality, for example, are often attained by restrictions laid on private users of these resources.) In this context, members of the community will have preferences about the levels of the various public goods produced by a community, and these will depend upon the benefits and costs, and the distribution of benefits and costs, associated with alternative levels of the public goods. These individuals, expressing their preferences through the political system, will determine the levels of production of the public goods.

This determination of the public goods output of a fixed community of residents, a specific example of the more general problem of collective choice via preference aggregation addressed by Arrow (1), Buchanan and Tullock (2), and Haefele (6), has been carefully examined by McGuire and Aaron (11).

The fixed-population assumption does not take account of the fact that populations do have some mobility. At any given time the level of public goods provision may differ substantially from community to community within a metropolitan region. Consequently, a household has the option to move to an area which more nearly meets its preferences for an optimum bundle of both public and private goods. This possibility is probably more important with respect to environmental quality than in regard to other public goods like education and police protection, since some environmental factors such as large landscape features and microclimates can be modified only to a very limited extent.

Public goods which are provided on a geographic basis, in particular by fixed communities, have been analyzed by Tiebout (21), McGuire (10), and Hamilton (8). These analyses fall at the opposite end of the spectrum from those based on fixed population. They have concentrated on the way in which households adjust by migration to the various public goods menus which different communities offer. This migration process, it is argued, results in a sorting out of households according to their preferences for public goods. In the extreme case, preferences within each community become identical, thus obviating the need for any collective decision-making mechanism.

Several earlier papers have looked at environmental quality as a problem for collective choice theory. The most recent is that of Haefele and Kneese (7), and that paper can be regarded as a takeoff point for this one. In it the authors provided a critique of the received (Tieboutian) doctrine of optimal jurisdiction which relies on "voting with the feet" and pointed out the need for a theory that takes account of both migration and collective decision processes.

In the present paper we explore more deeply some reasons why migration cannot be exclusively relied upon to result in the "optimal" provision of public goods. Furthermore, we try to take some steps toward a more complete theory of public goods provision, one which includes some elements of the supply side of the problem.

In the Haefele-Kneese paper, a suggestion was put forward that the collective choice problem associated with the provision of multiple public goods, in multiple overlapping jurisdictions, might be solved by something called "general purpose representation." We further explore and assess this possibility in the present paper and compare it with some alternative methods of preference aggregation.

We should be clear that our focus in this paper is on the provision of public goods in metropolitan regions and that this does not comprehend the entire environmental management problem. Air pollution, some aspects of water pollution, solid waste disposal, and the provision of public parks and open spaces are, by and large, metropolitan problems, on both the supply and demand sides. But major aspects of water management are not. Since upstream waste discharge, streamflow storage and regulation practice in upstream watersheds, and channel modifications all influence the quantity and quality of water at distant downstream locations, the water management problem usually reaches far beyond the boundaries of a metropolitan region. We do not address this problem here.

We turn now to discussion of why a collective decision-making mechanism (CDM) is needed in a model of local public goods provision in a metropolitan region, even where migration is possible.

THE NEED FOR A COLLECTIVE DECISION-MAKING
MECHANISM

Introduction

The Tiebout model of local public goods provision includes, as we have indicated, no role for a CDM. In fact, migration into and out of a large number of discrete communities is viewed as a way of avoiding the necessity for a CDM. This view is based on the notion that

67

household migration in response to the different menus of public goods which various communities offer will result in communities made up of residents with identical public goods preferences. Since the public service demands of the members of a community do often appear to differ, the logic of the Tiebout model supports a conclusion that conflicts with our view of the facts. Our interest in resolving this conflict prompts the following analysis of local public goods provision and household location decisions.

At the outset, it is important to be clear about the model we begin to develop in this paper. We are concerned with a metropolitan region partitioned into several communities. This region is assumed to be small enough that a household can live at any location within it and still commute to work at reasonable cost. Differences in the costs of commuting associated with differences in residential location will be ignored. There are several public goods which each community produces and provides to households within its boundaries. The cost of providing these public goods is met by a tax on the property within each community's boundaries.

This model can be regarded as embodying some rather standard assumptions in the analysis of local public goods provision, but it does abstract from some important aspects of reality. For instance, environmental improvement will often be obtained by laying restrictions on private firms. The distribution of costs within the community under such a regulatory approach will differ from the distribution that would obtain if the improvements were financed by property tax increases. Moreover, some, or most, of the cost may be shifted outside the community entirely. The model is, however, sufficient to demonstrate the necessity of a CDM.

In this model any household residing in a community is entitled to consume the local public good menu that community produces. Therefore, when a household rents or buys a dwelling, it also buys the right to consume the public goods provided in the community in which the dwelling is located. Consequently, local public goods are essentially bought and sold through the housing market. Households acting as consumers of residential services and public goods menus constitute the demand side of this market. Households acting as owners of residential property and as decision makers about community public goods production constitute the supply side.

In the context of this market structure, we will argue that the public goods demands of households within a community may differ and consequently that there will be a need for a CDM to resolve these differences. This will be true in both a short-run context, in which the housing stock in any community will be heterogeneous, and a long-run context, in which community housing stocks will tend to be homogeneous. Before doing so, let us examine in some detail the actions of households as consumers and suppliers of public goods.

The Demand for Local Public Goods

Households are confronted with a large number of residential alternatives. Within each community there may be several different kinds of dwellings, each of which provides the inhabitant with that community's public goods menu. Similarly, equivalent housing will be located in many different communities, and this will be supplied in combination with many different public goods menus. A household must balance its desire for a housing style and a public goods menu against the cost of satisfying those desires and choose a residential location which best satisfies its preferences.

The price per period of a dwelling is its rent. That is, rent is the price paid by the occupant for the services of the dwelling for one time period. This is true not only when the occupant and owner are different people, but also in the case of owner-occupied dwellings. In the first case, rent is an explicit payment from tenant to landlord. In the latter case, rent—the amount that would be received per period if the dwelling were rented out—is the opportunity cost per period of living in the dwelling instead of renting it out or selling it. It is an imputed charge paid from the household as a consumer of residential services to itself as producer of residential services.

Given the supply of residential alternatives offered in the metropolitan area and the market rents for these alternatives, the household as consumer makes a utility-maximizing residential choice for the present period. As indicated previously, this choice will involve the selection of a residential style and a particular public goods menu, the latter being a vector with a value for each of the variables such as public education, public safety, or air quality.

As an example, let us consider a household's choice with respect to air quality. In figure 1, indifference curve U represents the preferences of a household for air quality and a composite commodity we call "other consumption." This two-dimensional indifference curve is a cross-section of the household's total indifference surface with the values of all variables in the housing–public goods vector except air

69

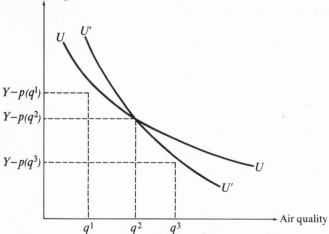

Figure 1

quality held constant at some given level. Suppose there are three identical houses in three communities which differ only with respect to their levels of ambient air quality. One house is in community 1, which has air quality q^1; one is in community 2, which has air quality q^2; and one is in community 3, which has air quality q^3. Let $p(q^1)$, $p(q^2)$, and $p(q^3)$ be the respective rents of the three houses, and let Y be the total income that the household can spend on both housing and other consumption in the present period. Y will be made up of labor income and the return on other productive activities engaged in by the household. If it owns its own dwelling, Y will also include the imputed income of that dwelling—its rent minus its tax.

The household has a choice between three levels of air quality. First, it could live in community 1, consume air quality level q^1, and spend $Y - p(q^1)$ on other consumption. Or, for a price of $p(q^2) - p(q^1)$ in foregone other consumption, it could move to community 2 and increase its consumption of air quality from q^1 to q^2. For an additional price of $p(q^3) - p(q^2)$ it could move to community 3 and increase its consumption of air quality to q^3. Therefore, the rent differential between the houses, which we have assumed to be identical in every respect except the air quality of their respective communities, serves as the price of incremental changes in air quality. Of course, this price may be different for different house styles or given different fixed levels of the other public goods.

70

Suppose the household lived in the house in community 1. As indicated by the indifference curve, the consumption benefit of an increase in air quality from q^1 to q^2—defined as the amount of other consumption the household is just willing to give up to increase its consumption of air quality from q^1 to q^2—is greater than the price of that increase. The household would therefore be willing to move to community 2. Consider now a potential move from 2 to 3. The amount of other consumption the household is willing to forego is less than its price and the household would be better off in 2.

As an approximation, the consumption benefit of a change in air quality from q^2 to q^3 for a household living in community 2 will be roughly equal to the difference in rent between its chosen dwelling and a similar dwelling in community 3. If it were more, the household would move to 3. On the other hand, if it were much less, the consumption benefit of the change from q^1 to q^2 would also likely be less than $p(q^2) - p(q^1)$ and the household would move to 1. The consumption benefit of a change from q^2 to q^3 can be approximated by MRS$(q^3 - q^2)$, where MRS is the marginal rate of substitution between air quality and other consumption evaluated at the air quality level q^2 and other consumption level $Y - p(q^2)$. Thus, MRS$(q^3 - q^2) \approx$ $p(q^3) - p(q^2)$ and MRS $\approx [p(q^3) - p(q^2)]/[q^3 - q^2]$. That is, the MRS of any household living in community 2 can be approximated by the air quality rent differential, $[p(q^3) - p(q^2)]/[q^3 - q^2]$, for dwellings of the type selected by the household. Hence, households that make similar residential choices will have similar public goods preferences. That is, their public goods marginal rates of substitution will be similar.

That is not to say, however, that their public goods preferences are identical. In the diagram, a household with income Y and preferences represented by the indifference curve U' will make the same residential choice as the household with preferences represented by U. Yet, the MRS's of U and U' at the air quality level q^2 and other "consumption" level $Y - p(q^2)$ are different. Hence, households making equivalent residential choices do not necessarily have identical public goods preferences. This results from the limited number of consumer alternatives available through migration. A household can consume only those public goods menus that are produced by existing communities. Given that there are only a finite number of communities, there will be only a finite number of alternatives. Only if there is a continuum of public goods consumption possibilities is it possible to conclude that individuals who make equivalent residential choices have identical public goods marginal rates of substitution. Otherwise, one can only conclude that at best the migration process tends to sort out households into groups with roughly similar public goods preferences.

The Supply of Local Public Goods

Households as owners of residential property are producers of residential services and public goods. The gross return per period for this production activity is the rent earned by the property—the amount a consumer must pay to live in it. The net return is the rent which the property commands minus the tax that must be paid on it.

The public goods menu in a community has two important effects on the net return earned by a dwelling in that community. First, the public goods menu is an important part of the consumption services supplied to occupants of the dwelling. Consequently, it influences the desirability of the dwelling from the viewpoint of consumers and hence the demand for it. The demand determines the price that consumers must pay per period to live in the dwelling—in other words, its rent. Consequently, the public goods menu supplied in a commodity influences the gross return on a dwelling in the community. Since the public goods menu will also determine the taxes charged in the community, it affects the net return on any dwelling as well.

Consider again the example of air quality discussed above. Suppose a proposal is introduced to improve air quality in community 2 by requiring industrial plants in the community to convert to production processes which reduce the emission of polluting agents into the atmosphere. As a result of this change, air quality in community 2 will improve from q^2 to q^3, the quality of air in community 3. Industrial plants are to be subsidized for this change, however, and these subsidies will be financed through an increase in property taxes in community 2.

An owner of a house in community 2 will evaluate the effect of this change in the following way: He will observe that houses identical to his in community 3 receive the rent $p(q^3)$. Since his house will be equivalent to such houses with respect to both residential services and the public goods menu after the change, he will expect his house to receive the same rent as identical houses in community 3, namely $p(q^3)$. In other words, because he ignores possible adjustments in other communities, his gross expected gain will be $p(q^3) - p(q^2)$. Suppose he expects his taxes to increase from t^2 to t^3 because of the subsidy. He will expect a net increase in his return if $p(q^3) - p(q^2)$

$> t^3 - t^2$. Therefore, when acting as a producer of housing services, he will favor the proposal if the change in his net return is positive.

In fact, this analysis of the household as producer of housing services also demonstrates the way in which public goods supply decisions are made in a Tieboutian world. That is, households observe the public goods menus of other communities in the metropolitan area as well as the rents which houses identical to theirs earn in these communities. Then, in an attempt to maximize the net return on their houses, they propose alterations in the public goods menu of the community in which they live. They obviously will favor increases or decreases in the level of provision of certain public services as long as the effect of such changes on their net return is positive. In this way, the many residents of each community affect the menu of public goods which each community supplies.

Favoring any change in the public goods menu is not such a clear-cut matter, however, if the household happens to occupy the dwelling it owns. In this case, the household acts as the consumer of that dwelling's services as well as the producer. This dichotomy is not troublesome if there are other communities in the metropolitan area with houses identical to the one the household owns and inhabits, and with public goods menus identical to the preproposal menu in community 2. Then the household would favor the increase in air quality if $p(q^3)$ − $p(q^2) > t^3 - t^2$ because it could sell or rent its house, move to an identical one in an identical community, and have more money for other consumption. In other words, there would have been no change in the household's consumption opportunities, and its disposable income would have increased. In such a circumstance where identical alternatives were available, a houseowner inhabiting his house would always favor proposals increasing the net return on it.

Suppose, however, that there is no equivalent to community 2. Then, if community 2 proposes a change in air quality from q^2 to q^3, the consumption possibilities of the household also change. In terms of air quality, the available levels would be restricted to q^1 and q^3 if the change were to be made. Moreover, even taking the increased income into account, it is not clear whether the household would be willing to move. It might instead be willing to forego the nominal income gain to consume air quality level q^2.

The purpose of this discussion is simply to argue that a houseowner may not always act as a return-maximizing producer when evaluating public goods proposals. In certain situations, it is perfectly rational for

73

a houseowner to consider a public goods proposal strictly in terms of his personal consumption benefits.

Consider now a household in the air quality example which owns a house in community 2 and evaluates the proposed change from q^2 to q^3 *strictly* in consumption terms. It will determine the amount of other consumption it is willing to sacrifice in order to increase its air quality consumption from q^2 to q^3. From the conditions of consumer equilibrium, this amount is roughly equal to $p(q^3) - p(q^2)$. If this amount is greater than the increase in taxes, $t^3 - t^2$, the household will favor the proposal; otherwise it will oppose it. As an approximation, then, a household will favor the proposal if $p(q^3) - p(q^2) > t^3 - t^2$. We have shown that a household acting as a producer of residential services will also favor the proposal if $p(q^3) - p(q^2) > t^3 - t^2$. Thus, the decision of a household with respect to a public goods proposal may not be much different if it acts as a producer or as a consumer of housing services.

Collective Decisions and Dynamic Considerations

The Short Run. In the short run the housing stock is in place, and community boundaries are fixed. In this context, the market value of a particular type of dwelling in communities with a certain public goods menu may be higher than its construction cost due to the scarcity of that combination of dwelling style/public goods menu relative to the demand for it. Similarly, due to the relative abundance of a certain dwelling style/public goods combination, its market value may be lower than the construction cost of the dwelling. This short-run context is of some practical importance since the construction of dwellings is likely to respond to market incentives with some time-lag. Also, once a dwelling is built, it requires relatively minor additional expenditures over time. Consequently it is not likely to be torn down just because its returns do not cover initial construction costs.

Consider now a community composed of several different styles of dwellings. Suppose, for example, a proposal is made to increase the level of expenditures on public education, to be financed by an increase in the educational tax rate. This proposal can be expected to increase both the rents and the taxes on dwellings in the community. For any dwelling style, the increase in property taxes will be some fixed proportion of the total increase in expenditures. This proportion is the ratio of its assessed value to the total assessed value of the community. There

74

is no reason to expect, however, that the ratio of the increase in rent on that style of dwelling to the tax increase will be the same for different dwelling types in the community. For instance, houses particularly suitable for families with children—those with three or four bedrooms and large lawns—may receive relatively large increases in rent due to the scarcity of the combination "child-suited house/high educational expenditures" relative to the demand for that combination. Houses not particularly suitable for families with children—townhouses, for instance—may receive relatively small increases in rent due to the relative abundance of the combination "child-unsuited house/high educational expenditures." Consequently, the sum of the rent increase minus the tax increase (i.e., the net return) may be positive for four-bedroom houses, and negative for townhouses.

As indicated in the section on supply, houseowners, whether acting as consumers or as producers, are likely to favor the proposal if the rent increase exceeds the tax increase and oppose it otherwise. Hence, owners of four-bedroom houses will be likely to support the proposal and owners of townhouses will be likely to oppose it. There will be a need, therefore, for a collective decision-making mechanism to resolve the disagreement.

The Long Run. In the long run the stock of housing capital will adjust to market incentives. The supply of any residential alternative will expand or contract according to whether the market price of this alternative is above or below its construction cost. As shown by Hamilton (8), who considered communities using zoning requirements to limit "fiscal externalities," these long-run movements will tend to result in communities with homogeneous housing stocks. Consequently, we are led to consider the need for a CDM when housing stocks are homogeneous.

If the housing stock in a community is homogeneous, both the rent and tax change resulting from a change in the public goods menu will be the same for all dwellings in the community. Consequently, if all houseowners evaluate the change in terms of its effect on the net return of their dwellings, their opinions concerning the proposal will be identical. Therefore, proposals would be accepted or rejected unanimously. However, as we have demonstrated, some households may find it in their best interests to evaluate public goods proposals strictly in terms of consumption benefits.

If the number of communities in a metropolitan area is small, the dichotomy between consumer and producer "behavior" will lead to differences of opinion about proposals, and hence even given the homogeneous housing stocks which zoning may encourage, a CDM will be necessary.

COLLECTIVE DECISION-MAKING MECHANISMS

In the previous section we demonstrated the necessity for a collective decision-making mechanism in a model of local public goods provision which allows for household migration. In the short run this CDM was necessitiated by the heterogeneity of any community's housing stock and hence the differential effect which changes in that community's public goods menu will have on the net return to houses within its boundaries; moreover, the discreteness of public goods menus, due to the likely limit on the number of communities in a metropolitan area, indicates that such a mechanism would be necessary even in the long run when housing stocks are variable and likely to be homogeneous in each community.

In this section we intend to consider alternative collective decision-making mechanisms in the context of our model of local public goods, a model especially concerned with the public good called environmental quality. We will concern ourselves with four CDMs, three of which are currently used to make collective decisions in the presence of conflicting individual preferences, and one which is similar to the concept of "neighborhood government."

Before we do so, however, we wish to comment briefly on an existing proposal for environmental management, which was one of the first undertaking to incorporate political factors. Dorfman and Jacoby (4) have formulated what they refer to as a "conceptual model of a regional water quality authority." They give the impression that their model will enable us to improve upon decision making by executive leadership—of which cost-benefit analysis is an example—because it provides a role for popular representation and hence the responsiveness of the collective choice to the preferences of groups of constituents in a river basin.

Essentially, the model is based on the selection of certain "Pareto-admissible decisions," i.e., vectors of policy variables which satisfy pertinent technological, political, and legal constraints and which result in a distribution of net benefits such that no individual could be made better off without at least one other individual being made worse off. Then, a set of "political weights," w_i, are chosen and the Dorfman-Jacoby problem becomes one of choosing that Pareto-admissible decision, X, for which

$$W = \sum_i w_i NB^i(X) \tag{1}$$

is maximized, where $NB^i(X)$ is the net benefit to individual i from decision X. It is at this point that the D-J formulation seems to us to converge to a cost-benefit analysis which considers a number of projects designed to achieve the same end and in which benefit recipients and cost bearers are assigned different weights.

We have some reservations about their formulation, the most important of which is that it seems to be not at all "political" in the common sense of the word. The weights to be used in the summation of net benefits are obviously of critical importance to the model, yet Dorfman and Jacoby give no indication of the way in which they are chosen other than to say that "we can often form a pretty fair judgment as to what they [the weights] are not" (p. 73). Furthermore, once several sets of weights are chosen as candidates for the final set, Dorfman and Jacoby give no indication of the way in which the members of the river basin authority (are they elected or not?) decide on the final set, and hence on the final decision, X. Do they vote by majority rule, unanimity, or what?

In other words, Dorfman and Jacoby do not go very far toward indicating the kinds of arrangements which certain groups of voters would make with others in an attempt to protect their interests. Such arrangements are caused by and illustrative of the varying intensities of preference of different groups over a set of independent issues or over the elements of a policy vector like X in the D-J model. Moreover, they should be the essence of any "political" model, it would seem to us.

We feel that these arrangements between voters have so much potential for resolving political and economic conflict that we will judge the four CDMs to be considered here primarily on the extent to which they facilitate such arrangements. Since these arrangements usually take the form of vote trades ("you support X for me and I'll support Y for you"), we are in effect advocating the exchange of votes. A growing literature supporting vote trading already exists[1] and we will not work through the analytics here, but a brief example may prove helpful before we begin our discussion of CDMs.

Consider the case of a community which has several different styles of housing and which must reach a decision on two separate issues; one issue might be an increase in educational expenditures and the other the construction of a park, both kinds of expenditures to be financed by increases in property taxes. Suppose now that there are a number of houseowners who stand to gain significantly from approval of the educational expenditure increase but that a majority of citizens will suffer slight losses because increases in their property taxes will outstrip the increase in the rents their houses earn. Suppose also that a minority of houseowners would benefit greatly from the construction of the park but that more citizens would realize slight net losses from the project. (Those living near the park might realize increases in the rent their houses would earn, which would outstrip their increased property taxes, while the opposite might be true for those living farther away.)

Since more people oppose each proposal than favor it, each would be expected to lose if voted on individually. Moreover, since we have postulated that the minorities are intensely in favor of passage and the majorities only slightly in favor of rejection, we see that many individuals lose on issues of great concern to them and win on issues of little concern. If agreements between voters could be made, however, 'some voters slightly opposed to the park but strongly in favor of the

---

[1] The desirability of vote-trading agreements is discussed by Haefele (6), Coleman (3), Mueller, Philpotts, and Vanek (14), and Buchanan and Tullock (2). However, both Riker (18) and Riker and Ordeshook (19) have argued against its desirability claiming, respectively, that it may lead to a diminution in the well-being of each voter and that it violates Arrow's condition of independence by irrelevant alternatives. These objections are discussed in a paper by Portney and Haefele (17), which makes other observations about vote trading as well.

While it is true that there is some question about the Pareto-optimality and stability of a vote-trading equilibrium *in a purely theoretical model*, we feel that the institutional structure of the "real" political world is such that vote trading is desirable. Factors like the continual change in the composition of the electorate, the introduction of new issues and the disappearance of old ones, and alterations in the preferences of voters violate the assumptions of purely theoretical models to such an extent that pessimistic conclusions derived from them ought not to be taken as a prima facie case against vote trading. In fact, since the "game" changes so much over time, there is reason to feel that gains ought to be maximized in each time period; we feel that vote trading does just that.

increase in educational expenditures might be willing to support the park. In exchange they would expect to obtain support on the education issue of citizens who were slightly opposed to it but who had a large stake in construction of the park. In such a way, large groups of voters could insure winning on issues of great rather than little concern to them. This is, of course, the appeal of vote trading. We turn our attention now to the way in which certain CDMs make possible such improvements.

Popular Referendum

Decision making by popular referendum is a method by which questions (most often about changes in expenditures and/or revenue raising) are placed on a ballot and put before the voters of a jurisdiction. The issue is decided by a simple majority of those voting. The popular referendum has seen its widest use for proposed increases in local property taxes to finance increases in educational expenditures. However, the use of referenda is not restricted to questions of education and property taxation, as witnessed by the increasing reliance on them to settle questions of environmental importance (see Portney [16]).

In spite of its apparently increasing popularity, popular referendum provides no means whatsoever for the expression of intensities of preference. Rather, voters are generally restricted to a "yes-no" decision with the result that those who would benefit or suffer greatly from a proposal have no way of distinguishing themselves from those who would benefit or suffer only slightly. Furthermore, popular referendum makes trades between voters virtually impossible. That this is so has been discussed elsewhere (see Jackson [9] and Buchanan and Tullock [2], for example). Briefly, such arrangements are most unlikely under a popular referendum mechanism because there are too many voters to facilitate the formation of majority "coalitions," i.e., the information requirements are much too large, and also because there is no way under popular referendum to insure that any kind of agreement which voters might make would be kept. Enforceability is impossible with secret balloting, and there is an incentive for each voter to enter into agreements with other voters but to "cheat" when it comes time to cast the vote he had promised to another.

We have of course "stacked the deck" in our example by positing intense minorities and apathetic majorities as well as by assuming that those in the majority differ from issue to issue. If the majority were

79

the same on all issues or if the majority were always as adamant as the minority, such trades would be impossible to arrange. Like Madison, however, we suspect that there are many instances in which some members of a relatively disinterested majority on one issue would be willing to make arrangements with similarly dispassionate majority members on another issue to insure their desired outcome on an issue about which they are greatly concerned but on which they are in a minority. For this reason, popular referendum seems a poor way of resolving the conflicts that inevitably arise in a system of local governments, even when migration is possible.

Multiple Representation

By *multiple representation* we refer to the practice by which the citizens of a jurisdiction elect different individuals to represent them on separate boards or commissions, each empowered to make decisions on a specific public good. For example, in some areas boards of education make all decisions concerning educational expenditures and revenues,[2] public safety commissions make similar decisions on police and fire protection matters, and public sanitation commissions decide questions of sewage treatment and garbage collection. Citizens are given the chance to elect members to these boards to represent their preferences, but the important thing to note is that each board has the single purpose of overseeing only one collectively provided service and hence each representative votes only on matters relevant to the board on which he sits.

As a result, multiple representation as a CDM suffers from the same defect that popular referendum does. Namely, multiple representation does not allow voters (or their representatives) to express intensities of preference over a set of independent issues. There is no way for a school board representative, say, to indicate that his "constituency" favors a certain proposal, but only in a lukewarm fashion; he can only vote his constituents' preferences.[3] Since he has a vote only on educational decisions, moreover, he cannot possibly arrange a trade or form

---

[2] When the property tax rate reaches some predetermined maximum rate per dollar of assessed valuation, increases in educational expenditures financed by tax increases must often be approved in a referendum. It is because the maximum rate has been reached in many places that we see boards of education losing their discretionary authority.

[3] This ignores the fact that school board representatives are generally elected on an at-large basis, not on a geographic basis. This makes the identification of "constituencies" most difficult, of course.

80

a coalition with a public safety commission representative, for example, *even though such a coalition based on intense minority interests may be desirable from the standpoint of many or all voters.* Where strong political parties exist, some implicit logrolling may take place in the formation of "slates" of candidates for the various single-purpose governments. This will be much less effective than explicit logrolling, however.

Multiple representation is very relevant to a model like ours, which tries to take explicit account of environmental problems, because several current proposals for environmental management are based upon the creation of water quality control boards or commissions that would have jurisdiction only over environmental problems. (See, for example, the work of Whinston and Ferrar [22] and Roberts [20].)

Multiple representation is unattractive as a CDM because it fails to provide a means by which voters or their representatives can bargain and coalesce over a number of issues in such a way that intense minority interests are sometimes satisfied. This is especially true when considering environmental preservation versus commercial or industrial development, for example, since environmentalists often constitute a particularly intense minority in the real world.

We turn our attention now to two CDMs that *do* facilitate the formation of agreements and, consequently, the occasional representation of such intense minority interests.

Geographic, or Metropolitan, Representation

Under a system of metropolitan representation, an entire metropolitan region would be divided into geographic districts of approximately equal population, and each district would elect a representative to a metropolitan government. Assume, for instance, in figure 2, that the

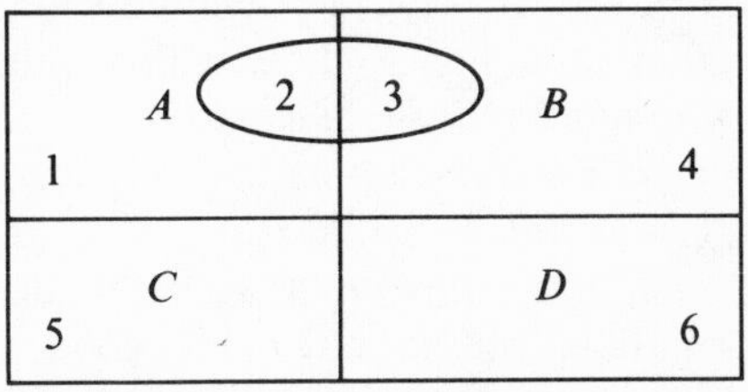

Figure 2

large square area represents an entire metropolitan region which is comprised of four smaller, square communities labeled A, B, C, and D. If it were decided that a metropolitan government should be formed,

81

each of the four communities might, for example, be divided into four precincts or wards and each of these wards might elect a representative. The metropolitan government would consist of these sixteen representatives plus any at-large representatives the charter might call for.

If we make the reasonable assumption that each of the four communities in our metropolitan region has a government of its own, why would such a metropolitan government be necessary? Clearly, such a government would be desirable if the communities decided that many of the serious problems facing them were areawide rather than specific to each of them. For example, the transportation network in a large metropolitan area is clearly best conceived of on an areawide basis rather than by each constituent community acting alone and in ignorance of, or even in opposition to, the plans of the others. Economies of scale make it necessary to take the larger view.

Such a view also seems desirable when considering the issue of the natural environment. First, in almost every conceivable instance an entire metropolitan area is included in a common watershed and generally in the same airshed as well. Therefore, improvements in air and/or water quality are important to all the communities in an area and, consequently, merit discussion at a higher level of government than the local. Also, environmental features like mountains, lakes, or forests are "natural" public goods (although impure because certain individuals must travel to enjoy their benefits) and often provide benefits which go across jurisdictional boundaries. When this is so, formulation of certain policies concerning the natural public good on a community-by-community basis may be suboptimal.

In figure 2 we have tried to illustrate this last point by including a hypothetical natural public good with somewhat elliptical boundaries. It might be a mountain, for example, and the issue might be whether or not to develop a public park on its slopes. Since the natural public good, and hence those individuals who are able to benefit from it without traveling, falls in two legal jurisdictions, some fragmentation in policies concerning the public good may result—that is, community A may favor a different course of action toward the natural public good than community B. If this disjointedness is troublesome, policies regarding the natural public good may be better decided at the metropolitan level of government. A similar conclusion might be drawn if a river formed the eastern boundary of communities B and D and if they could not agree on mutually satisfactory policies regarding ambient water quality.

In short, when considering air or water quality or natural public goods, noncoincidence of public goods boundaries with existing political boundaries may be sufficient to shift decisions to a metropolitan government, as may the existence of large-scale economies of the sort which exist in the case of public transportation. Since such boundary noncoincidence seems to be not the exception but rather the rule in large metropolitan areas, the existence of a metropolitan government appears to be a minimum condition for sound environmental policy.

We hasten to point out, however, that not all issues would have to be resolved at the metropolitan level. Decisions about education, police and fire protection, and sanitation have generally been thought to be the domain of the individual local governments and the existence of a metropolitan government for the resolution of certain problems would not vitiate the need for local governments to resolve local problems.[4]

The primary advantage of geographical or metropolitan representation is that it facilitates the kinds of agreements necessary to secure the mutual gains from trade discussed above. For simplicity, suppose that two proposals are before a simplified metropolitan government consisting of one representative from each of the four communities depicted in figure 2. The first proposal would provide for an increase in metropolitanwide expenditures on transportation, and the second would provide for increased expenditures for the enhancement of a natural public good, the boundary of which is indicated by the elliptical area in figure 2. Let us assume that many of the residents of communities A and B favor enhancement of the natural public good because it would increase their property value but that they oppose increases in transportation expenditures. Assume, however, that the former issue is of much greater concern to them than the latter. Likewise, we might expect the residents of communities C and D to oppose environmental enhancement, since none of them benefits directly from the natural public good, and we assume in order to make our point that they strongly favor increased transportation expenditures (such expenditures might,

[4] The classification of problems as local or metropolitan may be changing for a variety of reasons, however. The sheriff of Cook County, Illinois, has already proposed the abolition of city and suburban police forces in the Chicago area, to be replaced by a metropolitan police force. As concerns education, several recent court decisions (Judge Robert Mehridge's in Richmond, Judge Steven Roth's in Detroit) have indicated that educational inequality between central cities and suburbs, due to differences in fiscal capability, may be illegal and that remedy may lie in an integration of city and suburban school districts; this would, in effect, "metropolitanize" education.

for example, put their houses within commuting distance of a major employment center and hence increase the value of those houses).

Using a method derived elsewhere (Haefele [6]), we can represent these preferences and intensities in a simple way which clearly points out the possible gains from the exchange of votes. In figure 3 we

Issue	Representative			
	A	B	C	D
Transportation improvement	N_2	N_2	Y_1	Y_1
Environmental enhancement	Y_1	Y_1	N_2	N_2

Figure 3

have indicated that the representative to the metropolitan government from community A opposes the transportation expenditure increase (as indicated by the N for "no") and that he favors the environmental enhancement of the natural public good (Y for "yes"). The numerical subscripts indicate that environmental enhancement is more important to him than transportation improvement, however (he would rather see the environmental issue pass than see the transportation issue fail). The same preferences are held by community B's representative. Clearly, the representatives from C and D have opposite stands and intensities. If passage of any proposal requires the votes of three of the four representatives, both issues will clearly fail in the absence of agreements between the representatives.

However, if representative A is willing to switch his "no" vote on the transportation issue (about which he is little concerned) to a "yes" vote, then representative C, who intensely favors the transportation increase, would be willing to switch his vote on the environmental enhancement expenditure from no to yes. The result of such a trade would be three yes votes on each issue, and both would therefore pass. Obviously, if unanimity were required, representatives B and D could arrange an identical trade. When both issues pass, most voters find that their intense preferences have been satisfied—something that would not have happened if a popular referendum on the two issues had been employed or if an elected transportation board had resolved the one issue and an environmental commission the other. The advantage to such a metropolitan government is that it greatly increases information flows by reducing the number of decision makers on any question, thus enabling them to consider a wide variety of issues in a forum in which such vote trades can take place.

General Purpose Representation

Another response to the assumed suboptimality of governance by popular referendum or multiple representation has come from Haefele (5). This solution, referred to hereafter as general-purpose representation, is in many ways similar to the metropolitan form of government discussed in the previous section. We shall, therefore, briefly describe this proposal, point out its similarities to metropolitan representation, and discuss several important differences between general purpose and metropolitan representation.

Under general purpose representation a number of equal population districts would be drawn—Haefele suggests that congressional districts, state senatorial districts, or state representative districts could be used— and each such district would elect one general purpose representative. This individual would then represent his district on *all* the governing bodies which affect his district, e.g., the board of education, the planning commission, and the sanitary commission. This system would replace the one currently in existence whereby residents of such jurisdictions elect a *different* individual to represent them on each of the governing bodies which affect them, a system we have criticized earlier for its failure to provide a means of expressing and sometimes satisfying intense preferences.

Notice that a separate governing body would exist for each collectively provided service or function; in this respect general purpose representation resembles multiple representation and differs from metropolitan representation and its single governing body.[5] However, since each general purpose district elects but one individual to sit on each of many governing bodies, that individual can and most certainly would arrange trades with other general purpose representatives who sit with him on common governing bodies. Membership on common governments would probably occur frequently for any two representatives, and the trades they would make would of course reflect their constituents' intensities of preference over the issue space. In fact, several problems are likely to affect entire metropolitan regions—mass transit and ambient air and water quality, to name two—and in such cases all the general purpose representatives would have votes on those issues.

[5] Notice that up to this point the formulation of the general purpose representation mechanism is similar to Olson's principle of "fiscal equivalence" (see Olson [15]). While Olson's model is never cast in terms of representative democracy, his view is consonant with Haefele's feeling that the number of governments required under such a scheme would not be unmanageable. For an opposing point of view, see Mueller (12).

An example may help to highlight the similarities and differences between metropolitan and general purpose representation. Let us refer once again to figure 2 and make the following assumptions: (1) all the citizens of communities A, B, C, and D are commonly affected by air pollution; (2) a river forms the eastern boundaries of communities B and D, and proposals concerning the river affect only the residents of those two communities; (3) education is provided by all four communities; (4) the elliptical area is a park, and the residents of the area are under the jurisdiction of the park authorities.

Given these assumptions, we can divide the metropolitan region into "sectors," or areas in which each resident is governed by the same bodies. For example, the residents of sector 1 are governed by community A's school board and by the air quality board (we assumed that all residents are affected by air pollution). The residents of sector 2 are governed by A's school board, the park authority, and the air quality board. The residents of sector 3 are governed by community B's school board, the air quality board, the water quality board, and the park authority. Similarly, we can identify the governments which affect sectors 4, 5, and 6.

We can now compare the likely scope of a metropolitan government with a system of general purpose governments. Consider first the metropolitan government. If we assume that there is one representative from each of the four communities and that each of these representatives gets a vote in the single government on each issue affecting residents of more than one community, then each of the four representatives will get a vote on questions of air pollution (all communities affected), water pollution (communities B and D affected), and park administration (some residents in A affected and some in B). The matter of education we assume to be a purely local concern, and hence it is not considered before the single government. In figure 4 we illustrate what we

Issue	Metropolitan representative			
	A	B	C	D
Air	X	X	X	X
H_2O	X	X	X	X
Park	X	X	X	X
Education	—	—	—	—

Figure 4

shall refer to as the "voting rights" of each of the metropolitan representatives, where an X indicates that a particular representative has a vote on a particular issue.

We can demonstrate an analogous set of voting rights under a system of general purpose governments in which each government consists of only those representatives whose constituents are included in that jurisdiction. For example, if we considered each of the six sectors in figure 2 as a general purpose district, the matrix of voting rights would look like figure 5. Here we see that all representatives have votes in the air quality governing body. Similarly, only the representatives from sectors 3, 4, and 6 have votes on the water quality governing body (since the policies concerning the river are assumed to affect *only* communities B and D), and only the representatives from sectors 2 and 3 have votes on the park authority. The votes on education are bracketed to indicate that representatives 1 and 2 and representatives 3 and 4 can trade only with each other, since education is purely a local community matter.

In the interest of simplicity, we have considered an artificially small number of actors and issues. Surely a metropolitan government would have more than one representative from each community; moreover, we have assumed sectors to have approximately equal populations so that we could restrict the number of general purpose representatives. There are, in reality, many more kinds of jurisdictions in a real metropolitan region, and there would need to be substantially more than four general purpose governments. Nevertheless, we feel that our example points out several important differences between metropolitan and general purpose representation, and it is to a discussion of those differences that we now turn.

First of all, it should be clear that the vote-trading possibilities under a metropolitan form of government exceed those in a system of general

Issue	General purpose representative					
	1	2	3	4	5	6
Air	X	X	X	X	X	X
H_2O	—	—	X	X	—	X
Park	—	X	X	—	—	—
Education	$[X$	$X]$	$[X$	$X]$	—	—

Figure 5

purpose governments. To be exact, there are eighteen different possible trades that could be arranged, given the matrix of voting rights in figure 4 for the metropolitan government. However, only six vote trades are possible, given the allocation of votes described in figure 5, for general purpose representation.[6] If we view each possible trade as an opportunity for a representative to increase the likelihood of passage of an issue that is very important to his constituency, at the expense of relinquishing some control over an issue of little concern to them, metropolitan representation makes such opportunities three times as likely in this simple example. Since more representatives are likely to have votes on any given issue under a metropolitan form of government than under general purpose government, as we have defined them here, greater trading possibilities will exist under the former and it is to be preferred to the latter, on these grounds at least.

Restricting the voting rights of any general purpose representative to only those governments that have jurisdiction over his constituents has both a good and a bad effect. Let us first consider the latter. In those instances (probably rare) when a particular constituency is under the jurisdiction of a very small number of governments, their representative has very little to offer in a trade designed to satisfy an intense preference they might have. He has, in other words, nothing to offer in a deal. Refer to figure 5 for a moment. Sector 1's representative has only one possible trade to make—a trade with sector 2's representative on the issues of air quality and education. If it happened that the residents of sector 2 felt intensely about the same issue as the sector 1 residents, even this trade could not be arranged (both representatives would want to win on the same issue), and representative 1 would have no way of dealing to satisfy his constituents' intense preferences. Similarly, representative 5 can make *no* trades because he votes on but one issue and therefore has nothing to offer to attract the support of another representative. Migration may well be the response to a situation in which certain residents find themselves represented in but one government where their representative has nothing to offer to attract votes.

There is, however, an advantage to restricting representatives' voting

[6] Notice that we are discussing *possible* trades, not trades that would definitely be made. A possible trade exists when two voters have two issues in common. A trade will not take place, however, unless they have opposite stands on both issues and unless they are intensely concerned about opposite issues.

rights to those governments having jurisdiction over their constituents. Several writers, most notably Mueller (12) and Coleman (3), have raised the objection that vote trading may put certain traders in monopsonistic positions on specific issues, the result being that a trader may, as Coleman puts it, "gain more in utility from the set of decisions than his power may warrant" (p. 1118). In other words, a trader may have an interest in only one or two issues before a governmental body but may have voting rights on many issues that must be considered. This is undesirable, Coleman and Mueller feel, because it may lead to extortionate gains as the representative trades away his "free" votes on many issues to other representatives who are intensely interested in the issues to which those free votes may be applied. In other words, too many "pork barrel" projects would be approved.

To the extent that this is a serious problem, general purpose representation eliminates it altogether while metropolitan government may tend to foster it. Quite simply, no general purpose representative can vote in a particular government unless his constituents are under its jurisdiction and, presumably, are affected by it. If they are not under the jurisdiction of a governing body, their representative has no vote in it and, hence, has no free votes to bargain with. This is not to say that each constituency is intensely interested in all the decisions made by each of the governments having jurisdiction over it. Rather, it will be very concerned about some and little concerned about others; that is the essence of politics. What general purpose representation does is insure that each constituency has *some* interest in the decisions on which its representative has a vote. The opposite is likely to be the case with metropolitan government as we have conceived of it here. Since we have assumed that policies which affect more than one community are decided in the metropolitan government by the representatives of *all* the communities, free votes are likely to exist.

Whether the need for a collective decision-making mechanism in modern metropolitan areas would be best served by a metropolitan government or a system of general purpose governments depends on the seriousness of the drawbacks we have just discussed. Our suspicion is that while the "free vote" problem may be a serious one in state or federal governments because of the spatial separation of representatives' constituencies, it is not likely to be so in a metropolitan government. Problems or jurisdictions which affect more than one community in a metropolitan area are likely to affect the whole area or at least a large part of it. For this reason, most metropolitan representatives would be casting votes on issues of some concern to their constituencies. Monopsony power would be small. Conversely, as the issues under consideration in a system of general purpose governments begin to affect more and more people in the metropolitan area, the system of general purpose governments converges to a metropolitan government and all representatives vote on all except the purely local issues.

Given the greater likelihood of trading in a metropolitan government, the unlikelihood of a serious monopsony power problem due to free votes, as well as the savings in information and administration costs,[7] we prefer it to a system of general purpose governments. However, in a typically large metropolitan area the differences between metropolitan and general purpose representation are not likely to be significant. It should be clear that we regard either CDM as preferable to decision making by popular referendum or multiple representation.

CONCLUSIONS

We conclude that neither pure migration nor sole reliance on a CDM is adequate for the most effective aggregation of preferences for collectively provided goods in general and for environmental quality in particular. Both alternatives must be reflected in both descriptive and normative models of the processes involved.

We examined the recently proposed general purpose representative as a CDM device and compared it with three others. The criterion was how effectively these processes function to aggregate preferences and especially to reflect the strong preference of minorities on particular issues. The general purpose representative system seems clearly superior to referenda and multiple representation. Whether it is also superior to metropolitan government for dealing with the public goods problems of urban regions is, however, a very open question. General purpose representation does confine control of a collectively provided service to those individuals who are affected by it; this is to be preferred whenever possible. But in practice it may be very difficult to define which inhabitants of an urban region are, and which are not, affected by a public action. In addition, general purpose representation limits the scope for vote trading and thus the opportunity for expression of intense

[7] Since there are fewer governments to arrange and support.

minority interests in public goods issues in a metropolitan region. Our tentative conclusion is that metropolitan government is to be preferred. Effective preference aggregation with respect to public goods is extremely important if they are to be provided efficiently. In the absence of an effective CDM, voting with the feet may be the *only* alternative available to those with particular preferences for public goods including environmental qualities. Relatively homogeneous suburban communities and new towns may establish themselves, and the Tieboutian processes may seem to be operating with marvelously high efficiency. But this could be primarily a manifestation of the inability of populations to exercise effective collective preferences in their existing communities for high-quality air, public safety, open space, and other public goods. The extra, and unnecessary, social costs of the Tieboutian solution in terms of added transport and utility costs, unfavorable alterations of environment in the cities, disruptions of social groups, etc., could be very severe. Furthermore, the process of migration tends to lead to ghetto-type situations where, for example, rich and poor are strictly segregated and the poor do not get public goods.

We must be modest in stating our conclusions, for our model is still quite primitive. In regard to environmental issues, we have not, as mentioned in the introduction, dealt with CDMs and the management of very large natural systems, such as river basins. We have not taken explicit account of the fact that many environmental goods are provided by restrictions on private behavior and not publicly provided based on local tax systems. If local air pollution from a General Motors plant were to be curbed on the basis of a decision made by the city of Detroit, costs, in terms of increased car prices, would be borne across the nation. Also, we have not taken specific account of the fact that higher levels of government frequently lay restrictions on the range of local decision making either via direct controls or by altering the economic tradeoffs by means of outside subsidies.

Since our interest was in examining some of the behavioral and normative aspects of "pure" political systems, we do not apologize for certain omissions—for example, that in fact dollars vote and some parties in the existing collective choice process have much more information than others. But these are important considerations in designing actual strategies for dealing with environmental questions. They may, for example, speak for minimum national environmental standards or minimum national emissions charges even though in models such as ours these would inhibit local decision-making processes.

91

REFERENCES

1. Arrow, Kenneth. *Social Choice and Individual Values.* 2d ed. New Haven, Conn.: Yale University Press, 1963.
2. Buchanan, James, and Tullock, Gordon. *The Calculus of Consent.* Ann Arbor: University of Michigan Press, 1965.
3. Coleman, James. "The Possibility of a Social Welfare Function," *American Economic Review,* vol. 56 (December 1966), pp. 1105–22.
4. Dorfman, Robert, and Jacoby, Henry. "An Illustrative Model of River Basin Pollution Control," in *Models for Managing Regional Water Quality,* edited by Robert Dorfman, Henry Jacoby, and Harold A. Thomas, Jr. Cambridge, Mass.: Harvard University Press, 1973.
5. Haefele, Edwin T. "General Purpose Representatives at the Local Level," *Public Administration Review,* vol. 33 (March/April 1973), pp. 177–79.
6. ————. "A Utility Theory of Representative Government," *American Economic Review,* vol. 61 (June 1971), pp. 350–67.
7. Haefele, Edwin T., and Kneese, Allen. "Residuals Management, Metropolitan Governance, and the Optimal Jurisdiction," in *Representative Government and Environmental Management,* by Edwin T. Haefele, pp. 89–117. Baltimore: The Johns Hopkins University Press for Resources for the Future, Inc., 1973.
8. Hamilton, Bruce. "The Impact of Zoning and Property Taxes on Urban Structures and Housing Markets." Ph.D. dissertation, Princeton University, 1972.
9. Jackson, John. "An Exception to the Power and Importance of the Mean in Models of the Democratic Electoral Process," Working Paper 705–72. Washington: The Urban Institute, March 1972.
10. McGuire, Martin. "Group Segregation and Optimal Jurisdiction," *Journal of Political Economy,* vol. 82 (January 1974), pp. 112–32.
11. McGuire, Martin, and Aaron, Henry. "Efficiency and Equity in the Optimal Supply of a Public Good," *Review of Economics and Statistics,* vol. 51 (February 1969), pp. 31–39.
12. Mueller, Dennis. "Fiscal Federalism in a Constitutional Democracy," *Public Policy,* vol. 19 (Fall 1971), pp. 567–93.
13. ————. "The Possibility of a Social Welfare Function: Comment," *American Economic Review,* vol. 57 (December 1967), pp. 1304–11.
14. Mueller, Dennis, Philpotts, Geoffrey, and Vanek, Juroslav. "The Social Gains from Exchanging Votes: A Simulation Approach," *Public Choice,* vol. 13 (Fall 1972), pp. 55–79.
15. Olson, Mancur. "The Principle of 'Fiscal Equivalence': The Division of Responsibilities Among Different Levels of Government," *American Economic Review,* vol. 59 (May 1969), pp. 479–87.
16. Portney, Paul. "Cost-Benefit Analysis and Majority Rule." Paper pre-

sented at the Annual Meeting of the Public Choice Society, March 22, 1973, at Annapolis, Maryland.

17. Portney, Paul, and Haefele, Edwin T. "The Exchange of Votes: Some Theoretical and Empirical Observations." Unpublished manuscript.
18. Riker, William. "The Paradox of Vote Trading," *American Political Science Review*, in press.
19. Riker, William, and Ordeshook, Peter. *Positive Political Theory*. Englewood Cliffs, N.J.: Prentice-Hall, 1973.
20. Roberts, Marc. "Organizing Water Pollution Control: The Scope and Structure of River Basin Authorities," *Public Policy*, vol. 19 (Winter 1971), pp. 75–142.
21. Tiebout, Charles. "A Pure Theory of Local Expenditures," *Journal of Political Economy*, vol. 64 (October 1956), pp. 416–24.
22. Whinston, Andrew, and Ferrar, Terry. "Taxation and Water Pollution Control," *Natural Resources Journal*, vol. 12 (July 1972), pp. 307–17.

MARK SHAREFKIN & TALBOT PAGE

Industry influence on environmental decision making

INTRODUCTION

IMAGINE an airline, which produces trips with capital, labor, and noise as factors of production. Up until now noise has been an unpriced factor and the whole airline industry has adjusted to this free input. Now there is to be a socially chosen "effluent tax" on noise, by some sort of vote, legislative or referendum. The airline can do several things:

1. It can do nothing. "Let the people decide how damaging the noise is to their ears. We will act like competitive price takers, accepting whatever tax-price is given us."
2. It can write a letter to all its affected laborers and stockholders. "We are a convenient organizational device. We are polling you to find if all or nearly all of you have the same sensitivity to noise, suffering the same intensity of marginal damage. If so, you might like to establish an interest group and we can save you some organizational costs. Please write down your marginal damage on the enclosed card and return it to us, remembering to exclude indirect considerations, such as moving costs and temporary decline in the return on your equity if the tax is passed. The efficient social solution does not include these calculations."
3. It can do the same as in 2, with this change: "be sure to figure in your possible unemployment and decline in stock value. These may be short-run temporary losses offset by gains in the rest of the economy, but they are real losses to you. Vote your interests!"
4. It can write a letter to the employees and stockholders urging them to vote "no" and predicting dire consequences of the tax; and without

Both authors are Research Associates, Resources for the Future, Inc.

consultation or permission from the stockholders, it directs operating funds into political activity until marginal costs equal marginal benefits, from the managers' point of view. Instead of a black box responding to their preferences, the firm treats its workers and stockowners as target groups for vote magnification for the firm's or the managers' preferences.

Academic discussions of the political behavior of firms emphasize 1 and 2 as descriptively realistic and derogate 3 and 4 as simplistic. And academic discussants labor to distinguish their analysis from what they regard as popular mythology. Be it popular mythology or folk wisdom, widely held beliefs that 3 and 4 are the descriptively accurate categories have been embodied in an array of legislation aimed at blocking interest-group "distortion" of social choice processes. Thus state and federal laws prohibit corporate contributions to candidates' campaign chests, and the federal and many state governments require lobbyists to register and make public the sources and uses of their funds.

Our paper has its origins in the observations that (a) the issue of interest-group distortion of legislative and referendum social choices on environmental quality issues is of great and growing importance, that (b) the nature of environmental problems leads to striking imbalances in the resources available to and costs borne by interest groups typically on the opposite sides of environmental issues, and that (c) we need and do not have a sound normative approach to the governance of interest-group participation. California's Coastal Zone Initiative was almost defeated in a referendum vote; Washington State's mandatory deposit bottle bill was defeated in a referendum vote. In both cases industry opponents of these measures outspent environmental advocates of the measures by factors of 10 and more. In both cases, preelection polls and election results indicated that massive industry spending shifted a large fraction of the electorate from the pro to the anti side. Does interest-group activity distort electorate preferences, and hence distort election outcomes? How do we go about asking questions of this type?

In this paper we attempt to conceptualize the problem of interest-group participation with sufficiently descriptive realism to be applicable to real problems of environmental choice and with sufficient simplicity and generality to form a basis for policy discussions of the governance of interest-group participation. The components of the formalization are the following: (1) a normative standard to judge the outcomes of social choice processes; for the standard we take the criterion of economic efficiency; (2) an enumeration of the social choice processes to be considered: an ambitious program would take the choice process itself as a decision variable, but we will be considerably less ambitious and restrict our attention to a few alternatives; (3) a behavioral rule to determine the action of individual agents participating in the social decision process under any given social choice rule; (4) similarly, a behavioral rule guiding decisions of industry participants in the social choice process, a rule which allows for the possibility of changing the behavior of individuals—what we will call "vote magnification." And finally, as a guide to a realistic conceptualization of each of these components of the problem, we need a case study in which interest-group participation has been well documented. We have been assembling documentation on a number of environmental issues ultimately resolved by referenda. The best-documented thus far is California's referendum on Proposition 20, the Coastal Zone Initiative, and the paper is sprinkled with tentative generalizations gleaned from our work in progress on this case study.

So much for preliminaries. We turn to the development of each of the essential components of a model of interest-group participation in environmental decision making.

A NORMATIVE STANDARD

The best-known solution to the public goods problem, the Lindahl[1] solution, is shown in figure 1. The initial endowment is q_1^0 of the private good to Mr. 1 and q_2^0 to Mr. 2, with zero of the public good Q for each. An indifference curve for Mr. 1 is represented by u^1, and one for Mr. 2, by u^2. In the simple case of a linear production possibility frontier, the sides of a wedge with appropriate fixed angle $/ABC$ show possible cost-sharing arrangements for financing the public good. The Lindahl solution occurs when the wedge is rotated around B to the position where the tangencies line up (at Q_L).

Two well-known problems plague this solution: (i) In the large-numbers case—where there are many recipients of airplane noise—the levying of differential taxes is impractical (too costly), even when everyone reports his sincere marginal benefit schedule to the tax collector. In practice, it is necessary to resort to an equal tax–sharing scheme, to

---

[1] For one of many expositions see H. Aaron and M. McGuire, "Efficiency and Equity in the Optimal Supply of a Public Good," *Review of Economics and Statistics*, vol. 51 (February 1969), pp. 31–39.

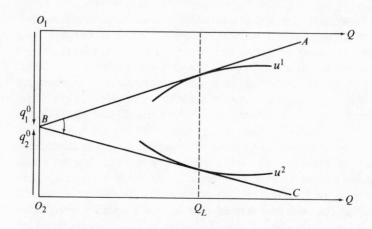

Figure 1

the tax scheme implicit in paying for the public good out of general revenues, or to whatever tax-sharing scheme is implicit in the adjustments necessary in producing the public good. (ii) In the small-numbers case, where the levying and collection of differential taxes is not prohibitively costly, the free rider problem is likely to be severe.

Problem ii we leave to the next section; our purpose in this section is to promote an efficiency standard less restrictive and more realistic than the Lindahl standard. Lindahl imposed two criteria: an aggregative requirement—that summed marginal rates of substitution of the public good for the private good equal the marginal private good opportunity cost of public good production, and an individual requirement—that marginal rates of substitution be equal to marginal tax prices.

$$\sum_{i=1}^{N} MRS^i(Q) = MC(Q) \qquad \text{aggregate requirement}$$

$$MRS^i(Q) = t^i(Q) \qquad \text{individual requirement}$$

If marginal benefit taxation is infeasible, then there is no way of satisfying the individual requirement. But what if we retain only the first criterion? The situation is summarized in figure 2. Individuals 1 and 2 do not agree on the amount of public good that should be given the tax-sharing arrangement, with individual 1 preferring a public good level $(\overset{*}{Q}{}^1)$ smaller than the quality $(\overset{*}{Q}{}_2)$ preferred by individual 2. Public good levels Q in the range $\overset{*}{Q}{}^1 \leqslant Q \leqslant \overset{*}{Q}{}^2$ will be preferred by both parties to public good levels outside of that range. Given any

98

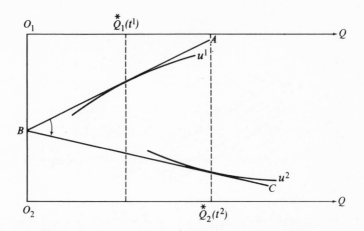

Figure 2

level in the preferred range, there will be no unanimous agreement to change, so that points in that range have a kind of stability. More important, at some point in the preferred range the first Lindahl criterion will be satisfied. That is the point that would be passed unanimously were side-payments allowed, and it is therefore the normative standard we take for assessing the outcome of a voting process under a fixed tax shares constraint when side-payments are prohibited. A social choice process constrained to a preordained tax share arrangement will be called efficient if it leads to this point, and inefficient if it does not.

A SOCIAL CHOICE RULE

The free rider problem remains. Is there some social choice mechanism available which circumvents this problem and leads to an efficient outcome? Reasoning from properties of that mechanism, we could analyze the normative significance of interest-group involvement by analyzing the impact of interest-group involvement on the social choice process.

There is such a mechanism, "median voting," and it seems to have been first described in Bowen's[2] classic paper. A very brief update of his paper can be compressed into a picture, figure 3, and a few words. There are N individuals, but otherwise the world is that of figure 1, with

[2] H. Bowen, "The Interpretation of Voting in the Allocation of Economic Resources," *Quarterly Journal of Economics*, vol. 58 (1943), pp. 27–48.

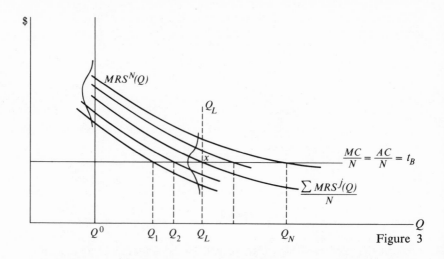

Figure 3

some initial distribution of private good income and a decision on public good production about to be made. Assume each individual's marginal rate of substitution $MRS^j(Q)$ between private good income and the public good is independent of income but dependent upon the level of public good—a reasonable assumption for marginal adjustments in noise abatement, in ambient air quality, or in noise level. Assume that the cost shares are fixed and equal (equivalent to assuming $\angle ABO_1 = \angle CBO_2$ in figure 2). Then the MRS^j curves of figure 3 can be drawn by plotting the slopes (figure 2) of the indifference curves along AB and BC (and other surfaces, for more people) in figure 2.

Bowen's argument is this: suppose that for any Q^0 the intersections of the curves $MRS^j(Q)$ with a vertical line through Q^0 are symmetrically distributed about the mean of the intersections. Now consider a median vote in which each individual writes down his preferred Q, this quantity being defined by the intersection of his marginal cost share (MC/N) and his MRS. Mr. 1 writes down Q_1 on his referendum ballot, Mr. N writes down Q_N. The social choice rule is that the median of these preferences, Q_L, is the public choice. Bowen's point is that at the efficient solution Q_L the mean of the curves MRS added vertically is on the cost curve MC/N (point x). Half of the MRS curves cut MC/N to the right of x and half to the left. Thus a vote which chooses the median of all preferences of Q $(Q_1, Q_2, \ldots, Q_N)$ will end up at the efficient choice x.

100

Bowen does not worry about strategic behavior. But that problem too is circumvented by the median voting rule. Voters who desire the median amount have no incentive to distort their true preferences. Voters who desire more than the median amount have no strategic incentive to report an unrealistically high desired quantity, because the median decision rule gives them no return from overstating their true preferences. Only reporting less than the median amount can change the outcome for someone with preferred Q greater than Q_L, but this would be self-defeating. The same argument, *mutatis mutandis*, applies to voters who desire less than the median amount.

The median vote equilibrium can be shown to exist by using the language of N-person game theory. Generalizing Bowen's equal unit tax price case to the case of arbitrary but foreordained individual tax shares $t^i(Q)$, a more realistic image of the tax system, consider figure 3. In the linear case, where the tax price is proportional to Q, each individual is tied to a utility function $U^i(q_0{}^i - t^iQ, Q)$, a one-dimensional reduction of his (ordinal) utility function $U^i(q, Q)$. Concavity of U^i (. . .) guarantees the concavity of $U^i(q^i - t^iQ, Q)$ with respect to Q, so that individual payoff functions are easily shown to be concave in individual strategies. Technology limits total public good output to that producible at zero private good output, so that we can take the individual strategy sets to be closed intervals $(0, Q_{max})$. Rosen's[3] work on concave games then assures the existence and uniqueness of a solution at the median sincere vote. For convenience define the N functions $U^i(Q) = U^i(q_0{}^i - t^iQ, Q)$, and note that for any given initial income distribution, these define N single-peaked preference scales, with respective peaks $\overset{*}{Q}_i(t_i)$.

Would a sequence of majority rule votes converge to this median voting equilibrium? Duncan Black's[4] work assures us that the median of the individual optima is the dominant alternative under ordinary majority rule. (This need not be identical with the median identified in Bowen's argument—when tax shares are different.)

In judging whether referenda are good or bad as a way of making the kinds of choices which concern us in this paper, much depends upon the relationship between the distribution among individuals of the private-good opportunity cost of producing the public good and the distribution among individuals of public good demand. Thus far the t^i have been

[3] J. B. Rosen, "Existence and Uniqueness of Equilibrium Points for Concave N-Person Games," *Econometrica,* vol. 33 (July 1965), pp. 520–34.
[4] D. Black, *The Theory of Committees and Elections* (London: Cambridge University Press, 1958).

simply written down and are available to further specification under various assumptions as to the factors influencing them: (1) capital ownership and employment in the affected industry, (2) the relative intensity of consumption of the affected product (for example, airline travel per individual), and (3) the marginal damage of the pollution itself. To go beyond heuristics, and more specifically to link effective tax prices of public good measures to claims on capital in the various industries, we must formalize the dependence of the t^is upon factors 1, 2, and 3.

INDIVIDUAL BEHAVIOR

Consider the case discussed above, in which a standard is to be imposed setting an upper bound upon a presently unrestricted public bad (such as airplane noise) which is simultaneously a factor of production. Passage of a binding standard[5] lower than the present noise level will affect individuals in four ways:

1. As consumers, individuals will face higher relative prices for airline trips.
2. Individuals who hold airline stock will suffer capital losses.
3. Assuming that all individuals value silence positively at the margin, all will gain from some noise abatement.
4. There may be temporary unemployment of workers in the polluting industry.

Each individual must weight those effects in arriving at his utility-maximizing referendum vote.[6] Define the variables:

$x_1{}^i$	i^{th} individual's consumption of the polluting good (good number 1)
$x_s{}^i$	i^{th} individual's consumption of the sth (nonpolluting) good, $s = 2, \ldots, M$
$\sum_{i=1}^{N} x_1{}^i = f(K_1, L_1, Q)$	production function for the polluting good industry
$\sum_{i=1}^{N} x_s{}^i = g_s(K_s, L_s)$	production function for the sth (nonpolluting) industry

[5] Standards are generally not equivalent to fees and usually introduce second-order inefficiencies. See T. Page, "Failure of Bribes and Standards for Pollution Abatement," *Natural Resources Journal*, vol. 13, no. 4 (October 1973), pp. 677–704. The type of inefficiency introduced by standards does not concern us here, however.

[6] We are assuming the referendum to be a median choice rule referendum.

$P_1(Q)$	price of the polluting good
$P_s(Q)$	price of the sth (nonpolluting) good, $s = 2, \ldots,$ M
Q	quantity of the public good
Y^i	i^{th} individual's private good income
K_s, L_s	capital, labor employed in s^{th} industry
r_s	rate of return on capital in s^{th} industry
$W^{(i)}$	individual's wage, equal to the wage in the industry in which individual i works; the superscript (i) means the industry in which i works; each individual is endowed with one unit of labor
$r_s K_s{}^i$	i^{th} individual's share of the return to equity in s^{th} industry

Then the ith individual picks his sincere referendum vote $\overset{*}{Q}{}^i$ by maximizing

$$U^i(x_1{}^i, x_2{}^i, \ldots, x_M{}^i, Q) \tag{1}$$

subject to the income constraint

$$Y^i(Q) = P_1(Q)x_1{}^i + \sum_{s=2}^{M} P_s(Q)x_s{}^i \tag{2}$$

Equations (1) and (2) are the usual statement of the individual's maximizing problem in terms of the usual (direct) utility formulation. More appropriate to our purposes is the indirect utility function, defined in terms of the direct utility function by

$$V(P_1, P_2, \ldots, P_M, Y^i, Q) = \max U^i(x_1{}^i, \ldots, x_M{}^i, Q)$$

$$\text{over } x_1{}^i, \ldots, x_M{}^i, \text{ subject to (2)} \tag{3}$$

The reason for the shift should be clear. We want to segregate price, income, and amenity effects on the individual's sincere vote, and the indirect utility function depends on just those variables. The individual's sincere vote is simply a parameter upon which the indirect utility function depends, both explicitly and implicitly, and the usual first-order condition for a maximum is $\partial V^i/\partial Q^i = 0$. Evaluation of the total differential gives

$$\sum_{s=1}^{M} \frac{\partial V^i}{\partial P_s} P_s' + \frac{\partial V^i}{\partial Y^i} \frac{\partial Y^i}{\partial Q} + \frac{\partial V^i}{\partial Q} = 0 \tag{4}$$

Dividing by the marginal utility of income and with slight rearranging, we have

$$\frac{\dfrac{\partial V^i}{\partial Q}}{\dfrac{\partial V^i}{\partial Y^i}} = - \sum_{s=1}^{M} \frac{\dfrac{\partial P_s}{\partial V^i}}{\dfrac{\partial V^i}{\partial Y^i}} P_s' - \frac{\partial Y^i}{\partial Q} \tag{5}$$

The lefthand side of (5) is simply the ith individual's marginal rate of substitution between income and abatement. The righthand side of (5) is the marginal tax "price" of abatement, and splits that effective tax price into M price effect terms and an income effect terms. Roy's formula

$$\overset{*}{x}_s{}^i = - \frac{\dfrac{\partial P_s}{\partial V^i}}{\dfrac{\partial V^i}{\partial Y^i}}, \ s = 1, 2, \ldots, M \tag{6}$$

(where $\overset{*}{x}_s{}^i$ is the $x_s{}^i$ demanded by individual i at his individual optimum) enables us to simplify the first M righthand-side terms of (5). Further, using the factor-side decomposition of the ith individual's income

$$Y^i = \sum_{s=1}^{M} r_s(Q)K_s{}^i + W^{(i)}(Q) \tag{7}$$

the derivative $\partial Y^i / \partial Q$ can be evaluated as

$$\frac{\partial Y^i}{\partial Q} = \sum_{s=1}^{M} r_s'(Q)K_s{}^i + W^{(i)'}(Q) \tag{8}$$

Substitution of (6) and (7) into (5) gives

$$MRS^i(Q) = - r_1'(Q)K_1{}^i - \sum_{s=2}^{M} r_s'(Q)K_s{}^i - W^{(i)'}(Q)$$

$$+ \overset{*}{x}_1{}^i(Q)P_1'(Q) + \sum_{s=2}^{M} \overset{*}{x}_s{}^i(Q)P_M'(Q) \tag{9}$$

as the equation determining the ith individual's utility maximizing vote. There are N such equations and N corresponding individual optima $\overset{*}{Q}{}^1, \overset{*}{Q}{}^2, \ldots, \overset{*}{Q}{}^N$.

104

Equation (9) is the point of departure for a discussion of the individual's voting calculus. Individual marginal rates of substitution of income for abatement are broken into four kinds of terms, or effects:

1. A portfolio term, the first term on the righthand side of (9), which registers the impact of abatement on the rate of return to capital into the polluting industry. (Capital is taken to be immobile between industries in the short run, so that individual industry rates of return differ between industries and in each case are determined by the requirement that the demand for capital equals the existing stock of capital.)
2. $M - 1$ portfolio terms, the second through M^{th} terms on the righthand side of (9), which register the impact of abatement on the rates of return to capital in all of the nonpolluting industries.
3. A labor income term, which counts the cost of abatement in terms of labor income forgone.
4. A set of price effect terms, which count the cost of abatement in terms of higher prices in the polluting industry and lower prices in the nonpolluting industries.

The lefthand side of (9) is the ith individual's marginal benefit evaluation of the last unit of public good. The righthand side of that equation is the effective marginal tax price he "pays," by the four effects listed above, for that marginal unit. We should expect these marginal tax prices to be increasing functions of Q, as they must be for individual optimum levels of the public good to be well defined. For example, consider the case of the airplane noise. The public good is silence, and passage of a noise standard amounts to a legislative decrease in the endowment of the factor "noise reception," a factor employed only by the airlines. Airline output is therefore relatively more intensive in this factor than the output of any other industry, so that short-run rates of return will decline in the airline industry and rise in all other industries.

$$r_1'(Q) < 0 \tag{10a}$$

$$r_s'(Q) > 0, s = 2, \ldots, M \tag{10b}$$

Similarly, the price of airline output will rise and the prices of output in all other industries will fall:

$$P_1(Q) > 0 \tag{11a}$$

$$P_s'(Q) < 0, s = 2, \ldots, M \tag{11b}$$

105

From (9), (10a), and (11a) it follows that passage of any higher noise standard amounts to imposing a positive effective marginal tax on all individuals, an effective tax increasing with their equity in airlines and their consumption of airline output. Similarly, the effects associated with stockholder equity in other industries and consumption of the output of other industries will be negative, but much more diffused.

In Bowen's case, marginal tax prices are assumed equal and constant for all voters, but his argument applies to our case in which "tax prices" are indirectly levied through the portfolio, wage, and price effect terms on the righthand side of equation (9). In our more general case, median voting gives an efficient outcome Q if the median $\overset{*}{Q}{}^{i}$ voter is also the voter with mean marginal rate of substitution equal to mean tax price at Q, and the tax prices need not be equal. A sufficient condition for efficiency is that the distribution of marginal rates of substitution be symmetrical, but the minimal requirement for efficiency in median voting is that the median fall on the mean.

Supposing for a moment that the median and the mean coincide, then median voting will lead to an efficient choice of the level of the public good as long as individuals can evaluate their own interests (the various terms on the righthand side of [9]). In other words, there is no need for industry interests to be represented explicitly by industry in the social choice process in order to achieve efficiency. These interests can be represented indirectly through individuals' evaluations of the price and other effects in (9).

In fact the industry interests most aggressively presented to the voter could perhaps be neglected altogether. These are the short-run effects of capital losses which the polluting industry might suffer. The short-run capital losses are more or less offset by short-run capital gains in the other industries. In any case the social decision might be better based upon the long-run price effects, leaving consideration of the short-run effects as problems of adjustment. Considerations of the long-run versus the short-run become immaterial if the social choice can be made often, so that the economy can increment slowly into the equilibrium (efficient) state, a process which washes away the short-run effects.

However, in a world where information is costly and where organized interest groups work to shape an informational environment, our individual voter may have trouble computing each term of (9) and voting his best interests. In the process of helping individual voters decide what is best for themselves, the economic interests may seek their own ends. We need a way of incorporating producer behavior into our model.

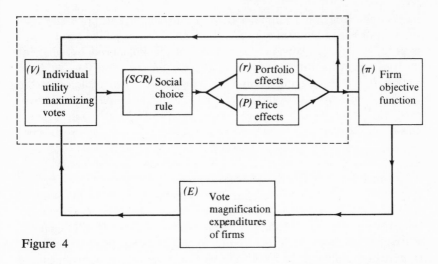

Figure 4

PRODUCER BEHAVIOR

Figure 4 charts the interdependencies among the components of a closed model, and suggests one way of introducing producer behavior. The dotted lines isolate the portion of the chart discussed in preceding sections. The purpose of this section is to sketch a specification of the portion of the chart outside the dotted lines, and thus to close the model. Square V, the component of the model to which we have devoted the most attention, stands for equation (9) or its equivalent. Square SCR, "Social choice rule," corresponds to the choice of a ballot format and of a method of aggregating individual ballot entries into a social choice of a public good level Q. There are many possible specifications of SCR, but in what follows, as in the previous discussion, we consider only one—"median voting"—in which individuals mark a desired noise level on their ballots, and the social choice is the median of the ballot entries. That social determination of noise level in turn changes rates of return and prices, and those changes are symbolized by squares r and P respectively. Those changes are considered by utility-maximizing individuals in casting their ballots, so that we have drawn a feedback line running from squares r and P back to square V. But changes in rates and return and prices are also data to firms making expenditure decisions, whence the line linking squares r and P with square π. Square π corresponds to some choice of producer objective function; in what follows we have chosen (expected) profit maximization, but other specifications can be explored. Finally, individual voting decisions are

107

based upon individual estimates of portfolio, labor, and price effects—these have been identified above—which any level of public good Q will impose. But those individual estimates will be influenced by what industries spend in order to influence those estimates, and thus we have square E, "Vote magnification expenditures of firms." Choice of the word *magnification* is suggested by the following description of an interest-group strategy for "buying" votes when actual cash transfer purchases are forbidden: move as many voters as possible inside your "natural" constituency by persuading them that what is good for you is actually good for them, i.e., "magnify" your natural constituency.

Turning to the actual specifications, assume that firms in the sth industry spend an amount E_s on vote magnification, with that amount determined by (expected) profit maximization. Let $p_s(E_s, Q)$ be the sth industry's subjective probability estimate that a standard Q will be passed when the industry's trade association spends E_s in appeals to the electorate to vote either a very low standard or a very strict one, depending on the standard's effects on its profits. Then that industry's expected postreferendum return on equity is

$$E[\pi_s(E_s)] = \int_0^{Q_{max}} p_s[E_s, Q][r_s(Q)][K_s - E_s] dQ \qquad (12)$$

Each industry's optimum expenditure is then determined by the usual first-order condition

$$\frac{\partial E[\pi_s(E_s)]}{\partial E_s} = 0 \qquad (13)$$

Note the simplifying assumptions implicit in this formulation: each industry's advertising expenditure is determined by its own judgment of the referendum's prospects for passage and by its own decision calculus, and is independent of any other industry's expenditure decision.

Why haven't we chosen a more general formulation? There are at least two directions of possible generalization deserving of passing comment: (1) a model of industry expenditure E_s which explains the sharing among firms of overall industry expenditure, and (2) a model in which each industry's vote magnification expenditure depends upon every other industry's vote magnification expenditure: for example, the sth industry's subjective probability estimate can be taken as $p_s(E_1, \ldots, E_s, \ldots, E_M, Q)$, much as firm advertising budgets in the cigarette industry are determined, in part, by rivals' advertising.

1. The intraindustry sharing of the costs of vote magnification again raises the free-rider problem. Since a referendum outcome favorable to a particular industry is of value to all firms in the industry, each firm in the sth industry has an incentive to minimize its own contribution to the industry campaign chest. In the event of a favorable outcome, each firm can hope to ride freely on the benefits that outcome confers on the industry. There is some evidence that this conundrum drives industries to explicit cost-sharing arrangements. We have obtained data on contributions by independent distributors to the National Soft Drink Association, a trade association which has lobbied Congress for an antitrust exemption useful in promoting throwaway containers. The highest contribution, $3,285, was made by ten of approximately seventy contributors, and twelve of the seventy contributors made contributions within a dollar of $515. The probability that these are random events is very small.

2. Organization cost arguments suggest that $E_2, \ldots, E_M$ are zero. In our airplane noise example the airlines have much to lose, but no other single industry has very much to gain: postreferendum rates of return $r_1(Q)$ in the polluting industry may differ substantially from the common prereferendum rate of return r in all industries, but postreferendum rates of return $r_2(Q), \ldots, r_M(Q)$ in the nonpolluting industries will not differ much from r. It follows that those industries have little incentive either to learn what other industries are spending or to respond in kind with expenditures of their own. Moreover, a coordinated campaign of all nonpolluting industries would impose substantial additional costs upon these industries, since organization for political action is typically on an industry basis. The contrast with the polluting industry is worth drawing: the organizational machinery for coordinated action in opposition to the referendum proposal is already in place, and the additional costs of such opposition to a specific proposal are correspondingly lower. In summary, the nonpolluting industries' expenditures $E_2, \ldots, E_M$ should be relatively small, and the polluting industry's expenditure E_1—determined by equation (13)—should be relatively large.

Translation of that expenditure figure into vote impact requires the specification of what we have called a vote magnification function. That specification should be guided by plausible hypotheses regarding industry appeals to the electorate. One way to generate such hypotheses is to start with natural "target" groups, groups likely to be sensitive to industry appeals. Stockholders are perhaps the prime target group: they are identifiable—in fact, they are known—and they can be appealed to on

109

the basis of their equity in the industry. Next in line are individuals as consumers of industry output, who are likely to be sensitive to the possibility of higher prices. Finally, there are the industry's employees, a group generally smaller in size than either the stockholder or the consumer group, but nevertheless a group with a major stake in any decision affecting industry employment. (In the fight over the supersonic transport, the fate of a few thousand jobs was a major talking point for a project generally conceded to be inefficient and widely believed to be potentially disastrous.)

We can therefore formalize the vote magnification process by attaching weights, or "effectiveness coefficients," to the portfolio and price terms on the righthand side of equation (9). Equation (9) is thus recast as

$$MRS^i(Q) = - \phi_1 r_1'(Q)K_1{}^i - \psi^{(i)} W^{(i)\prime}(Q) + \gamma_1 \overset{*}{x_1}{}^i(Q)P_1'(Q)$$

$$- \sum_{s=2}^{M} \phi_s r_s'(Q)K_s{}^i + \sum_{s=2}^{M} \gamma_s \overset{*}{x_s}{}^i(Q)P_s'(Q) \qquad (14)$$

If one of the weights is unity, then the corresponding portfolio or price term enters undistorted into the equation determining the individual's utility maximizing vote. If, for example, ϕ_1 is much greater than one, then the polluting industry has been successful in distorting individual assessments of possible portfolio damages upward.

Equation (14) describes individual voting behavior. Three kinds of interpretations of the weights are compatible with that description:

1. The ith individual's preferences have been changed, and equation (9), calculated in terms of that individual's new utility function, will give the same utility maximizing vote as equation (14) calculated in terms of the individual's old utility function.
2. The ith individual's preferences have not been changed, but he has become better informed during the campaign. The weights in equation (14) are the weights necessary to guide that equation to a solution at the better informed vote.
3. The ith individual has been deceived about the probable consequences of a referendum result unfavorable to the polluting industry, and the weights in equation (14) guide him to a vote which is not in his best interest.

Because the behavioral consequences of these three interpretations are identical, economists have tended to treat such distinctions as excess baggage, and if our only interest were in explaining individual behavior this would be a sensible attitude. But in a world in which knowledge and information often are power, in which the market for information is highly imperfect, and in which there are often large returns to investments in deception, it seems overly narrow. The distinctions can in fact be empirically tested. Ex ante claims can be compared with ex post outcomes. It may be hard to distinguish between intentional and unintentional deception, but in many cases it is possible to distinguish between accurate and misleading information. Moreover, there are policy implications to these distinctions. Public intervention can be designed to test information for its quality and to decrease its deceptive use, as for example in truth-in-lending legislation. Because the aggregate stake in reasonable outcomes in environmental decision making can be enormous, the question of deceptive information must be faced.[7] Distributors of nonreturnable containers spent several million dollars to defeat a Washington State mandatory deposit bill; initial polls indicated easy passage, and industry brought consumers over to their position with predictions of dire consequences if the bill were passed. A similar bill passed in Oregon has had no such dire consequences. (Incidentally, there is a move in California towards a measure of information equity in referendum campaign spending: Proposition 9, on the ballot in the 1974 election, forbids an expenditure disparity of greater than $500,000 between "Yes" and "No" campaigns.)

The ϕs, ψs, and γs should be taken as dependent upon industry campaign expenditure E. A few words on the forms of those dependencies: clearly over some initial range of expenditure

$$\phi_E > 0, \psi_E > 0, \gamma_E > 0 \qquad (15)$$

where subscripts indicate partial derivatives; otherwise there would be no public relations firms paid to make appeals to stockholders. Equally clearly, there are diminishing returns to campaign expenditures: too much spending can be counterproductive. The inequality in equations (15) will be reversed for some E, as many have found to their grief. One upper limit is imposed by the perils of visibility. There seems to be a threshold level of campaign expenditures beyond which the scale of vote-buying activity becomes offensive to the electorate, so that vote

---

[7] See G. Tullock, "The Economics of Lying," in his *Toward a Mathematics of Politics* (Ann Arbor: University of Michigan Press, 1967).

buying itself becomes a major campaign issue. Something like this probably happened in the vote on California Proposition 20. Whittaker and Baxter, the public relations firm retained by the No coalition, ran a high-visibility and well-financed campaign; the level of spending eventually led people to question their credibility.

With the above apparatus we can speculate upon efficiency aspects of actual referendum voting. First of all, a referendum ballot usually presents the voter with an up-down choice between some prescribed amount of a public good (perhaps an environmental one, as in Proposition 20) and no public good. For example, a school bond proposal may give the voter a choice between a $200,000 bond and no construction money. If it is a once-only referendum, then each voter must decide whether he prefers the $200,000 bond to no bond and vote accordingly. But if he knows that should the referendum fail, the following year the school board will come back with a referendum for a $180,000 bond (a figure designed to capture more votes), he may vote against the original $200,000 bond. As the time period between such referenda shortens, the process converges to the median one described above.

And secondly, preferences are unlikely to be symmetrically distributed in the way assumed by Bowen. In the airline example, noise is a bad so that the tail of the distribution of marginal rates of substitution is chopped off by the x axis. On the other side there are likely to be sensitive people with very high preferences for silence. Instead of looking vaguely normal, the distribution of MRS is likely to look more lognormal, with the tail pointing up. And as long as the distribution of MRSs is skewed so that the mean will be vertically above the median, then a median referendum will yield a Q lower than the efficient solution Q_L.

Starting out with a median referendum solution likely to be too low, consider the effects of industry participation. These effects, because of the asymmetry of organization costs, the concentration of potential short-term losses to the polluting industry, and dispersal of gains throughout the rest of the economy, are likely to push the referendum choice further away from the efficient standard Q_L.

If we treat all nonpolluting industries as one large second industry, then equation (14) becomes

$$MRS^i(Q) = - \phi_1 r_1'(Q) K_1{}^i - \psi^{(i)} W^{(i)'}(Q) + \gamma_1 \overset{*}{x}_1{}^i(Q) P_1'(Q)$$

$$- \phi_2 r_2'(Q) K_s{}^i + \gamma_2 \overset{*}{x}_2{}^i(Q) P_2'(Q) \qquad (16)$$

112

From equations (10a) and (11a) it follows that if either $\phi_1 > 1$, $\gamma_1 > 1$, or both (while the ϕ_2 and γ_2 are merely one), individuals perceive a tax price that is too high and therefore vote $\overset{*}{Q}{}^i$ that is too small.

In the other case, where the referendum is costly and time consuming and "recontracting" may not happen at all, there are interesting strategic considerations. For example, a school board may try to design a bond issue so that it will pass at 55 percent because it attaches a cost to a referendum defeat and is uncertain as to when there will be another referendum chance. Such considerations quickly get us beyond the simple apparatus set up above. The actuality is somewhere between the two extremes of multiple (costless) referenda for the same issue and only one referendum with no second chance. Thus our observations have to be tempered by the realization that referenda are in fact costly and time consuming. There is nevertheless some validity in the popular belief that industry influence in public choice can misallocate resources in an efficiency sense.

PROPOSITION 20

Over the years California beach open to the public shrank from 1,062 miles to 200 miles.[8] The amount of accessible public beach can be taken as a public good, and "saving" the remaining coast became a popular issue over the whole state. In 1970 two conservation bills were introduced in the state legislature: a liberal Democratic one and a milder Republican version which allowed for more local control. Lobbyists for the conservationists tried to get a compromise bill which could pass both the assembly and the senate. But the liberal bill died in committee in the assembly. The Republican bill moved from the assembly to the senate, where it was killed without a hearing.

The 1970 elections were considered favorable to the conservationists, who formed the Coastal Alliance soon after the elections in order to try again for a conservation bill in the legislature. This time the bill (Assembly Bill 1471) was supported by Assembly Speaker Robert Moretti and other prominent state legislators. The Coastal Alliance pushed hard for the bill, with Ansel Adams's posters, 1,400 local organizations, and a willingness to compromise in the legislative rewriting of the bill. While, according to the polls, the bill was overwhelmingly popular in the whole

[8] J. Adams, "Proposition 20," *Syracuse Law Review,* vol. 24 (Summer 1973), pp. 1018–46.

state, it was strongly opposed by utilities, developers, oil companies (who feared restrictions on offshore drilling), and construction companies. There were hearings and compromises in the assembly, and finally the bill passed, 56 to 17, in that house and was sent to the senate, where it was referred to the senate natural resources committee. There it died by one vote. (A possible swing vote by a senator from a southern California district, which was polled to be 73 percent for the bill, was never cast because the senator was out of Sacramento buying race horses.)

Twice rebuffed, the conservationists decided to try once more in the legislature but to be ready to push for a referendum if they failed again. New, un-watered-down, uncompromised bills were introduced in both the assembly and the senate, and a short version of the un-watered-down bill was readied for a referendum initiative. The assembly bill speedily passed and went to the senate, where it died along with the senate bill. The Coastal Alliance then began its referendum campaign.

The referendum campaign was a story of canvassing versus media. The anti-20 coalition outspent the Coastal Alliance twenty to thirty times. While the initial popularity slipped considerably (from an early 80 percent), the initiative passed by 55.1 percent.

In the conventional wisdom of social choice theory, referenda are considered generally bad. The argument is that though there may be some implicit vote trading in the drafting of a referendum proposal, there cannot be the full vote trading of the legislative marketplace, and that potential gains from the trade are thereby lost. The argument is plausible in a world in which legislators faithfully represent the preferences of their citizen constituents, so that legislatures are devices for reducing the organizational and informational costs of vote trading among individuals; it is unassailable in a world of two vote traders or two vote-trading blocks. But it is less persuasive in a real political world. Access to the referendum as a last resort is one check on the imperfections and power imbalances which the committee systems introduce into the legislative market. Referenda, or even the threat of referenda, can help keep the system more responsive to the electorate's preferences, as in the case of Proposition 20. A reader[9] of an earlier draft of this paper remarked that two of the states considered best governed by political scientists, California and Oregon, have constitutions which provide relatively easy access to the referendum.

[9] We are grateful to Roger Noll for this and other comments.

It seems to us that the inflexibility of referenda, which prevents most vote trading, may be an advantage as a social choice rule in some kinds of environmental decision making. After a vote-trading session in the legislature it is impossible to uncover an aggregate intensity measure (such as the sum of these marginal damages) by looking at a single environmental issue in isolation. The outcome of the legislative vote is determined in part by legislators' intensities on other issues. We must look at all the votes traded to find out how much was given up for what. Instead of trying to untangle the intensities of all the votes simultaneously in a whole legislative session, it may be simpler to obtain a direct reading of the electorate's preferences on a single environmental issue. The marginal rates of substitution of the environmental good for the tax price, unadulterated by strategic behavior on other issues, do have normative value. And a referendum, by not allowing voters to become traders, permits us to take the voters' pulse on a single issue at a time.

CONCLUSION

In some ways the theory of social choice has closely followed the theory of competitive markets. One of the underlying normative ideas in social choice theory is that social choices should be a consumer sovereignty of the polling booth in which social choices are based on individual preferences. Interest groups fit into a competitive market of political decision making the same way advertising fits into a market for private economic goods. Interest groups contribute, the traditional theory goes, by taking advantage of economies in scale in generating and disseminating information. The political process improves as voter-sovereigns on both sides of an issue form interest groups and improve informational quality. Political parties fit into a theory of political choice the same way firms fit into a theory of the competitive market—as black boxes which react passively to the preferences of voter-consumer-sovereigns. But how do firms fit into the political process? That is the question we attempted to address in this paper.

The reason for our interest in environmental decision making is that for this type of social choice, firms tend to line up on one side of the issue and private citizens on the other. One way of thinking about industry participation in political decision making is to consider firms as black boxes passively reacting to the preferences of their stockholders. In this view, the firm is no more than a convenient organiza-

115

tional device, saving the actual interest group (made up of the consumer-voter-stockholders) the trouble of organizing on their own. And in this view company political activity, per se, is benign, although firms' advantages in organizing interest groups might lead to some imbalance.

A decade ago some organization economists gave up the black box model of the firm in the economic marketplace. Their replacement was the "managerial firm," which is a large and growing organization managed by people who, in part, pursue their own objectives, exercise discretion, and are not simple maximizers of stockholder welfare. Correspondingly, just as a managerial firm may do more in the economic market than passively react to prices and costs, it may do more in the political market than passively react to the wishes of stockholders to the end of conveniently saving them organization costs.

In this paper we have taken a small step toward incorporating the firm into political choice theory. We have not invoked discretionary power in the hands of the firms' managers or the divergence of the managers' and shareholders' goals. In the model developed here, firms are still black boxes maximizing profits over the opportunities open to them. (We can see from equation [9] that maximizing a firm's profits is not the same thing as maximizing stockholders' welfare. There is an aggregation problem in going from the N conditions of equation [9] to some definition of stockholder welfare.) We have broadened the opportunity set a little, allowing political opportunities as well as the traditionally assumed private market economic ones.

What we have done, in the spirit of the managerial economists, is to complicate the flow of causality. Instead of assuming a unidirectional causality from voter preferences to political decisions, we have assumed that voter preferences imply potential outcomes of prices and profit rates which firms anticipate and react to. In an effort to maximize profits they in turn influence the way voters perceive the issue at hand. Thus the flow of causality feeds back upon voters; the process is no longer unidirectional, and there is room for efficiency distortions.

Sometimes the question of industry influence upon the political process is viewed as a question of equity. The outcome of political choice may be influenced by the endowment of individual preferences and the endowment of voting power, linked through stock ownership and corporate organizing capabilities. Viewed in this light, the problem of industry participation is an ethical one, and one traditionally avoided by economists. We are suggesting that the problem, in some of its aspects, is "simpler" than the ethical one of equity. In some of its aspects it is a question of efficiency, capable of being analyzed with the conventional tools of the trade.

To the extent that our model is realistic, there are policy implications to be drawn on efficiency grounds:

1. There is a case, based on efficiency, for sealing off the political process from economic producers. This means more than prohibiting corporations from making political contributions in elections (already the law) and in referenda (a possible reform). It also means that industry representatives should not have decision-making power in environmental standards–setting conferences or in regulatory commissions. This change, of course, would be a sharp departure from tradition. In the past, commissioners have been chosen for their industry background to insure that the "industry point of view" was represented. The policy implication from our model is that all the commissioners should be consumer representatives without industry loyalty. Industry expertise should indeed be solicited and could be solicited in the hearing process. Industry information would have to carry weight, not because of friendly commissioners with industry backgrounds, but on its own merits, as it reveals to consumers and consumer representatives the tradeoffs in equation (9).

2. If economic agents are to be included in the political process, perhaps because it is believed that they produce some accurate information along with the deceptive information or perhaps because there is no way to exclude them, then there is a case for providing a better parity of informational resources on the opposite sides of issues. This is particularly important when industry groups are lined up on one side of an environmental issue and individual citizens are on the other side.

3. It is worth thinking about ways of creating incentives so that the informational flow is less distorted. Insuring that there is a forum for the other side allows a chance for rebuttal to fraudulence. The fairness doctrine played a crucial role in the passage of Proposition 20, in eroding monopoly power in the information market. We do not need a better fairness doctrine; what we do need is a better way of implementing the one we have.

VICTOR G. ROSENBLUM

The continuing role of courts in
allocating common property resources

CONSTITUTIONAL AND OPERATIONAL CONTEXTS
FOR JUDICIAL ROLE

SOME CONCLUDING observations from a recent casebook for undergraduates on the Supreme Court's policy role might serve as a useful introduction to this assignment:

The salient fact is that in major substantive and procedural areas of constitutional law the Supreme Court has been a powerful political force performing multiple political roles.

This reality is what makes perplexing the admonitions of distinguished justices like Frankfurter and Harlan in *Baker* v. *Carr* that the Court should maintain "complete detachment, in fact and in appearance, from political entanglements" and abstain "from injecting itself into the clash of political forces in political settlements." Its very designation as a wielder of "the judicial power" by Article III of the Constitution was bound to make the Court a vital force in the formation and implementation of national policy. . . .

In sum, the Constitution made the justices neither philosopher-kings nor robots, neither charismatic leaders nor eunuchs; rather it provided powers coordinate with the other major branches of government through which their strengths, fallibilities, and aspirations as human beings and conscientious judges could be manifested.[1]

In essence, courts play key roles in establishing, reviewing, construing, and challenging public policies. These roles have been molded within contexts of constitutional language and tradition that stressed

The author is Professor of Law and Political Science, Northwestern University. The author is indebted to Suzanne Torrey, a third-year law student at Northwestern, for her valuable research assistance.

[1] Rosenblum and Castberg, CASES ON CONSTITUTIONAL LAW: POLITICAL ROLES OF THE SUPREME COURT (1973).

separation of powers and checks and balances as major means for enabling government to control the governed and, at the same time, obliging it to control itself. The framers of the Constitution insisted that the ability of government to perform its necessary functions depended not simply on having sufficient power to control its subjects but on the capacity to restrain itself within its proper sphere as well. Controls *over* government were components of effective democratic rule equal with controls *by* government.

By seeking to separate the impulse to take action from the opportunity to carry it out and by pluralizing initiatives as well as constraints through coordinate institutions of legislature, executive, and judiciary, the framers of the Constitution endeavored to energize creativity while controlling abuse.

Within this framework, the courts have functioned both as restrainers of power and as innovators or architects of policy. For example, it was the courts, not the legislatures, that imposed upon the nation the "separate but equal" standard for construction of the Fourteenth Amendment, emasculating efforts of the amendment's framers to end racial discrimination. *Plessy* v. *Ferguson*,[2] a late nineteenth century sample of judicial creativity, reinvigorated apartheid in America and shelved for at least two generations the Fourteenth Amendment as constitutional protection against racism. Reinterpretation of the state action concept by the courts during the 1940s expanded vastly the Fourteenth Amendment's protective range, illustrating once again how judicial initiatives, far more than those by legislatures or executives, cast the legal framework for race relations in the United States long before the decision in *Brown* v. *Board of Education*.[3]

Courts do not serve predominantly as innovators, however, if only because the limits on their efficacy are so apparent. As Alexander Hamilton noted in the *Federalist Papers*,[4] the judiciary has "neither force nor will, but merely judgment." Partly because they must rely on others for the implementation of decisions, and partly because decision-making traditions limit their enthusiasm for blazing new policy trails, courts function more typically and effectively as guardians of access and of fairness or process than as creators of policy.

Three myths have remained prevalent over the years in the folklore surrounding the judicial process. One is that the role of judges is confined to finding the law. The second, the antithesis of the first, is that

[2] 163 U.S. 537 (1896).   [3] 347 U.S. 483 (1954).   [4] No. 78 (1787).

judges are all-powerful in the formulation of policy. In actual practice, of course, judges both find and make law. They find, in precedents from the past, guides to the resolution of conflict in the present; but since immediate problems are rarely identical with those of the past, the opportunity to make law through selection and construction of precedent is available as well.

The third myth is the myth of efficacy. It assumes that knowledge about what law *is* is synonymous with knowledge of *how* people behave. Since in practice declarations by judges may be no more than admonitions as to how people *ought* to behave, it is essential that observers of the judiciary not be deluded into unseemly expectations about the impact of judicial decisions. That we observed in May, 1974, with school segregation still rampant, the twentieth anniversary of the Supreme Court's decision outlawing racial segregation in the public schools should heighten resolve to separate recognition of the existence of legal norms from assertion of their efficacy.

Roscoe Pound's classic *Introduction to the Philosophy of Law*[5] continues to require attention a half-century after publication because of the clarity with which he punctured judicial myths and sought the realities of judicial role. Pound focused on judicial concerns with the ends of law: helping the peace in a given society, maintaining general security through the security of social institutions, and making possible the maximum satisfaction of wants. A key empirical difference between then and now is that our wants have increased vastly and our resources for fulfilling them have declined. One consequence for judicial role has been that supervision of criteria and methodologies for allocation of common property resources has become a primary judicial function. Substantive policies are invalidated infrequently unless the methodologies or processes giving rise to them have been found deficient. Deficiencies can consist of overt denials of due process or of more penumbral failures to balance relevant competing interests fully before reaching particular conclusions. The typical weapon of today's judiciary when deficiencies are found is remand for further proceedings to the agency accorded jurisdiction.

This is not to say that courts have placed a moratorium on their capacity for innovative policy-making thrusts. The frequency of such role assertion has declined vis à vis supervision of agency processes but the capacity remains. The Supreme Court's decisions of December,

[5] (1922).

121

1973, in *Bonelli Cattle Company* v. *Arizona*[6] and in *Zahn* v. *International Paper Company*[7] offer salient examples. *Bonelli* formulated a federal standard over previously accepted state standards for a significant facet of resource allocation, and *Zahn* demonstrated the continuing power of the judiciary to decide who may have access to the federal courts to seek redress for damages from the misuse of common property resources.

RECENT PROTOTYPES OF JUDICIAL POLICY MAKING: BONELLI AND ZAHN

The power of the courts to allocate common property resources, and to determine who can have access to the judiciary's allocative machinery and under what circumstances, was reiterated with certainty in these two decisions. Unlike the majority of recent cases, which have been devoted to judicial review of legislative or administrative agency decisions, these dealt primarily with the validity and construction of judicial norms and processes.

In its assertion of the primacy of federal law, the *Bonelli* case reminds one of Justice Marshall's decision in *Gibbons* v. *Ogden*[8] almost a century and a half earlier. The Court ruled in *Gibbons* that it was not for the state of New York to dispose of navigation rights on the Hudson River and that, consequently, the monopoly granted to the Fulton Steamboat interests by the New York legislature was illegal. Since commerce was held to include navigation, Marshall maintained that the allocation of navigation rights came under the commerce clause of the Constitution and was a matter to be decided by federal law.

The current Mr. Justice Marshall ruled in the *Bonelli* case that federal law, not state law, governs the ownership of land abandoned by the stream of the Colorado River as a result of federal rechanneling projects.[9] This decision reversed the Arizona Supreme Court's earlier ruling that state law governed ownership.

The facts of the case are complex, but they must be delineated if the reasoning behind the decision is to be grasped. A parcel of land abutting the east bank of the Colorado River was conveyed by federal patent to the Santa Fe Pacific Railway Company in 1910, two years before Arizona's admission to the Union. Between the time of the land grant

---

[6] 42 U.S.L.W. 4080 (U.S. Dec. 17, 1973).
[7] 42 U.S.L.W. 4087 (U.S. Dec. 17, 1973).
[8] 19 U.S. 448 (1821).   [9] *Supra*, n. 7, at 4085.

122

and 1959, when the river was rechanneled, the Colorado moved slowly eastward, eroding the east bank and submerging the land in question. When the Bonelli Cattle Company acquired title to the original Santa Fe grant in 1955, all but sixty acres were covered by water. In 1959 the federal Bureau of Reclamation deepened and rechanneled the Colorado River, as a result of which its stream was confined to a much smaller portion of the Bonelli property. Bonelli filed suit in 1962 to quiet title to the land from which the river had withdrawn.

The state of Arizona argued that, as successor to the federal government to title to the river bed pursuant to the Equal Footing Doctrine[10] that became applicable on admission of the state into the Union, it held sovereignty over the land in question as a result of the erosion that had submerged it. After the state trial court and court of appeals upheld Bonelli's claim to the land, the Arizona Supreme Court reversed.[11] The decision was based in part on the state supreme court's interpretations of the Equal Footing Doctrine and the Submerged Lands Acts[12] of Congress, and in part on state law concerning avulsive change. It held that the state's ownership extends to the high water mark of the river, which was fixed by the natural state of the river as it existed in 1938 before the construction of Hoover Dam. Because the federal rechanneling project was "an engineering relocation of the waters of the river by artificial means," the consequent alteration did not affect the applicability of state law of avulsive change and did not remove title to the newly exposed land from the state.

Justice Marshall began his analysis of the case in the U.S. Supreme Court's decision with the assertion that the first issue to be decided was whether federal or state law governed the controversy. The Equal Footing Doctrine required that as new states were forged out of federal territories, they had to be admitted with the same rights, sovereignty, and jurisdiction as the original states. This meant that title to lands beneath navigable waters passed from the federal government to the new states upon their admission to the Union. The Supreme Court had ruled in *Oklahoma* v. *Texas*[13] that state title to the bed of a navigable river follows mechanically the river's gradual changes in course. This was deemed necessary in order that the states could guarantee full public

<hr/>

[10] *See* Joint Resolution No. 8, To Admit the Territories of New Mexico to the Union on an Equal Footing with the Original States, S.J. Res., 62d Cong., 1st sess. (1911).
[11] Arizona v. Bonelli Cattle Company, 108 Ariz. 258, 495 P.2d 1312 (1972).
[12] 43 U.S.C. §1301 *et seq.* (1953).   [13] 268 U.S. 252 (1925).

123

enjoyment of the navigable waterways. The Submerged Lands Act of 1953,[14] according to Marshall, confirmed the states' preexisting rights in the beds of waterways within their boundaries. Consistent with the common law doctrine concerning title to the bed of a river that has shifted course, the federal government abandoned, through the Submerged Lands Act, all federal rights to title to lands beneath the navigable streams as "hereafter modified by accretion, erosion, or reliction."[15] Although he recognized the Supreme Court's 1917 ruling, in *Arkansas* v. *Tennessee*,[16] that it is for the states to determine the rights of riparian owners in the beds of navigable streams belonging to the states, Marshall held that the issue before the Court was not what rights the sovereign state has accorded private owners in its lands, but rather "whether the State retains title to the lands formerly beneath the stream of the Colorado River and whether that title is defeasible by the withdrawal of those waters."[17]

Marshall then proceeded to refute the state's argument that the Equal Footing Doctrine supported its claim to the disputed land. He denied that the Equal Footing Doctrine was ever intended to donate to a state thousands of acres of dry land exposed when the main thread of a navigable stream was changed. The only circumstance under which a state could retain title to land from which a navigable stream had receded was when "the land was exposed as part of a navigational or related public project of which it was a necessary and integral part or when the artificial accretion was somehow caused by the owner himself."[18] Thus, had the rechannelization project been undertaken to maintain Arizona's title to the subject lands in order to protect navigation or to serve other related public goals, the state's claim to the land could have been upheld. In the absence of such a showing, the federal common law doctrine of accretion was held to govern the situation.

Three sentences focusing on policy rationales, rather than on technical legal norms, summed up Marshall's decisional approach: "The advance of the Colorado's waters divested the title of the upland owners in favor of the State in order to guarantee full public enjoyment of the watercourse. But when the water receded from the land, there was no longer a public benefit to be protected; consequently, the State, as sovereign, has no need for title. That the course of the recession was artificial, or that the rate was preceptible, should be of no effect."[19]

---

[14] *Supra*, n. 12.   [15] *Supra*, n. 6, at 4081, 43 U.S.C. §1301(a)(1)(1953).
[16] 246 U.S. 158 (1917).   [17] *Supra*, n. 6, at 4082.   [18] *Id.*, at 4083.
[19] *Id.*

In short, federal common law of accretion[20] prevailed as a result of the Court's acknowledged "analysis of the interests of the State and Bonelli, in light of the rationales for the federal common law doctrines of accretion and avulsion."[21] The weighing and balancing of policy interests, rather than the dictates of statute or other explicit legal norm, led to the conclusion that the state's retention of the land, once the waters receded, was unnecessary and unrelated to navigational protection, interstate boundary determination, or other significant public purpose. "The State's acquisition of the exposed land here could only be a windfall. . . ."[22]

Marshall saw the Court's role as analyst and applier of "accretion theory,"[23] which "guarantees the riparian character of land" by automatically granting to a riparian owner title to lands forming between his present holdings and the river and which, through their formation, threaten to destroy the valuable riverfront feature of his property.[24] The applicability of accretion theory was deemed reinforced by the fact that riparian owners may suffer noncompensable losses through exercise by the state or federal governments of their extensive powers over navigation.

In concluding his opinion for the 7–1 Court, Marshall intimated that since there was no claim by the state that depriving Bonelli of title to the land was necessary to any navigational or related purpose, the state's

---

[20] Federal common law has also been applied to resolving interstate pollution controversies. Illinois v. City of Milwaukee, 406 U.S. 91 (1972), a unanimous decision written by Mr. Justice Douglas, recognized a cause of action in aggrieved states under federal common law of nuisance for pollution of interstate waters by units of another state. The decision appears also to provide authority for the maintenance of suit in federal district court by individuals aggrieved for abatement of nuisance to their land arising from pollution of interstate waters. The Supreme Court declined to exercise its original jurisdiction, however, relying on the availability of an alternate forum. In denying the motion by Illinois, the Court remanded the case to the appropriate federal district court as an adequate forum to resolve the issues before it. See *Environmental Law— Cause of Action Under Federal Common Law for Pollution of Interstate Waters*, 77 DICK. L. REV. 451 (1973); *Federal Common Law in Interstate Water Pollution Disputes*, 1973 U. ILL. L. FORUM 141 (1973); *Illinois v. City of Milwaukee: Federal Question Jurisdiction Through Common Law*, 3 ENVIRON. L. 267 (1973).

[21] *Supra*, n. 6, at 4084.

[22] *Id.*

[23] *Id.*, at 4083. Federal law recognizes the doctrine of accretion whereby the "grantee of land bounded by a body of navigable water acquires a right to any gradual accretions formed along the shore." Hughes v. Washington, 389 U.S. 290, 294 (1968); Jones v. Johnston, 59 U.S. (8 How.) 15, 156 (1955).

[24] *Supra*, n. 6, at 4085.

assertion of title might violate the due process clause of the Fourteenth Amendment as a "taking without compensation."[25]

Justice Stewart, the lone dissenter, complained that the ruling that federal common law governs the resolution of conflicting claims to the exposed bed of a navigable river "emasculates the Equal Footing Doctrine" and is "wholly wrong."[26] Relying on the Court's exposition of the Equal Footing Doctrine in *Mumford* v. *Wardwell*[27] and its application of the doctrine in *Hardin* v. *Jordan*[28] and in *Arkansas* v. *Tennessee*,[29] Stewart concluded that the upshot of the majority's decision was that Arizona could be treated as "a second class State."[30] Were the Equal Footing Doctrine properly applied, he maintained, Arizona's sovereignty over the beds of navigable rivers within her boundaries would include "the power of the Arizona courts to decide this controversy under State law" and, consequently, "to decide it in a way that we here might think is wholly wrong."[31]

Having enlarged the scope of the federal courts' power and responsibility in the allocation of riverbed land that is later exposed "by the vagaries of the river"[32] or even by deliberate rechanneling by the federal government, the Court proceeded in its very next decision, *Zahn* v. *International Paper Company*,[33] to restrict access to the federal judiciary by claimants in class actions. With Brennan, Douglas, and Marshall dissenting, the Court ruled that each plaintiff in a class action suit must satisfy the $10,000 jurisdictional amount, and any plaintiff who does not must be dismissed from the case.[34]

Petitioners filed suit in federal district court on behalf of a class that, in addition to themselves, included some two hundred lakefront property owners and lessees around Lake Champlain in Orwell, Vermont. They charged International Paper with having discharged pollutants from its

---

[25] *Id.*   [26] *Id.*, at 4086.

[27] "The shores of navigable waters and the soils under the same in the original States were not granted by the Constitution to the United States but were reserved to the several States. . . . The new States since admitted have the same rights of sovereignty and jurisdiction . . . as the original States possess within their respective borders." 73 U.S. 423 (1968).

[28] "It depends on the law of each State to what waters and to what extent this prerogative of the State over the land under water shall be exercised." 140 U.S. 370 (1891).

[29] "How the land that emerges . . . shall be disposed of as between public and private ownership is a matter to be determined according to the law of each State." 246 U.S. 158 (1918).

[30] *Supra*, n. 6, at 4087.   [31] *Id.*   [32] *Id.*, at 4084.   [33] *Supra*, n. 7.

[34] *Id.*, at 4090.

pulp- and paper-making plant in New York into Ticonderoga Creek, which were then carried by that stream into Lake Champlain, causing damages to the value and utility of the surrounding properties. Convinced "to a legal certainty" that not every individual owner in the class had suffered pollution damages in excess of the $10,000 jurisdictional amount required for suits in federal district courts between citizens of different states, and concluding that it would be impracticable to define a class of property owners each of whom had more than a $10,000 claim, the district court refused to permit the suit to proceed as a class action. The Court of Appeals for the Second Circuit affirmed by a split vote, and the Supreme Court granted *certiorari.*[35]

In his decision for the six-man majority, Justice White stressed that the rule limiting suits between citizens of different states in district courts to those in which "the matter in controversy" exceeds the statutory minimum of $10,000[36] must be construed to forbid aggregation of claims in class actions whether or not any of the claimants otherwise satisfies the jurisdictional amount. He interpreted the Supreme Court's earlier opinion in *Snyder* v. *Harris,*[37] in which none of the named plaintiffs or the unnamed members of the class alleged claims exceeding $10,000, to mean that the Court "unmistakedly rejected" the proposition that amendments to the jurisdictional rules, adopted by Congress in 1966, were intended to effect any change in "the meaning and application of the jurisdictional amount requirement insofar as class actions are construed."[38] Especially in the absence of some express statement by Congress that it intended to depart from earlier statutory requirements and court interpretations, the Supreme Court was obliged to agree with the court of appeals that "one plaintiff may not ride on another's coattails."[39]

The dissenters viewed *Snyder* v. *Harris* as requiring only that there must be at least one plaintiff or joint interest seeking more than the statutory $10,000 amount in order to establish federal court jurisdiction over the controversy. Because Congress, since 1789, has said nothing about the requirements applicable to individual claimants but has prescribed simply that "the matter in controversy" must exceed a particular sum, it is consistent with both statute and precedent to conclude that jurisdiction over additional similar claims and parties is appropriate once jurisdiction has attached to "the matter." To deny such ancillary

---

[35] *Id.,* at 4087–88.   [36] 28 U.S.C. §1332(a)(1966).
[37] 394 U.S. 332 (1969).   [38] *Supra,* n. 7, at 4090.   [39] *Id.*

jurisdiction will not only impair substantially the ability of the prospective class members to assert their claims, said Brennan. It may also enlarge the federal judiciary's burden, "ironically reversing the Court's apparent purpose," by requiring separate litigation even by the individual plaintiffs meeting the $10,000 jurisdictional requirement.[40]

The dissenters relied also on "practical reasons" for permitting adjudication of the claims of all in the original class action, once the threshhold jurisdictional amount has been met. "Class actions were born of necessity. The alternatives were joinder of the entire class or redundant litigation of the common issues. The cost to the litigants and the drain on the resources of the judiciary resulting from either alternative would have been intolerable."[41] Difficult scientific issues calling for extensive use of expert testimony should not have to be probed repeatedly in different judicial forums when they can be definitively resolved in a single one. The chief influence mitigating what would otherwise have to become a flood of litigation by the more than two hundred claimants in the case—the fact that the cost of asserting many of these landowners' claims on a case-by-case basis will exceed their potential value—"will do no judicial system credit."[42] Brennan ended his dissenting opinion with the comment that the Court's curtailment of access to the judiciary through class actions "is both unwarranted and unwise."[43]

The least one can glean from these two most recent Supreme Court statements bearing on allocation of common property resources is that panaceas are alien to the judiciary. Litigants who anticipate systematic, efficient, consistent processing and disposition of their claims at the hands of the courts would have to believe as well in Santa Claus, the Stork, the Shmoo, and the Tooth Fairy.

Bonelli won after eleven years; Zahn and colleagues learned after three years that they could have no federal court access through class action. Practical considerations governing accretion seemed a major decisional factor in Bonelli; common sense rationales governing class actions influenced only the dissenters in Zahn. The Bonelli decision sought to expand federal jurisdiction and authority; Zahn to contract it. Bonelli rewarded the persevering individual who doggedly pursues his rights against the almost overwhelming claims of the state; Zahn shunted aside the damaged parties who couldn't show that their injuries from pollution of the lake by a corporate giant exceeded $10,000 in each and

---

[40] Id., at 4092.   [41] Id.   [42] Id., at 4092–93.   [43] Id., at 4094.

every instance. That no one has yet developed a foolproof means for assuring judicial consistency or for predicting the outcome of litigation is what keeps the legal profession in the highest ranks of the employed and maintains applications for legal education at their all-time high. But lest this dimension of judicial role induce cynicism or smugness, let me proceed to the more typical cases involving judicial supervision of administrative agency allocations of common property resources. We should find there more definitive and consistent patterns in the implementation of judicial role.

INTERPRETIVE ROLE PATTERNS IN JUDICIAL OVERSIGHT OF ADMINISTRATIVE AGENCY ACTIONS

The judiciary's role has been manifested in relation to agency allocative decisions primarily through cases that delineate guidelines for public access to information, those that construe the scope and methodology of agency actions pursuant to enabling statutes such as the National Environmental Policy Act,[44] and those that review agency rate-making functions and processes.

The Supreme Court's 1973 decision in *Environmental Protection Agency* v. *Mink*[45] offered a candid, though complex, view of information access. Rulings by the high Court justices in *Overton Park*[46] in 1971 and in *SCRAP*[47] in 1973 focused on the scope of considerations of environmental impact required of agency decision makers. Conceptions of methodology to be followed were probed thoroughly by the court of appeals in *Calvert Cliffs*[48] in 1971 and *International Harvester*[49] in 1973. Two Federal Power Commission cases, *Chemehuevi Tribe*[50] and *Mobil Oil*[51] in 1973, illustrated complementary judicial approaches to licensing

[44] For a comprehensive review of the operation of NEPA and its interpretation in the courts, *see* ANDERSON, NEPA IN THE COURTS (1973).

[45] 410 U.S. 73 (1973).

[46] Citizens to Preserve Overton Park, Inc. v. Volpe, 401 U.S. 402 (1971).

[47] United States v. Students Challenging Regulatory Agency Procedures, 412 U.S. 669 (1973).

[48] Calvert Cliffs Coordinating Committee, Inc. v. Atomic Energy Commission, 449 F.2d 1109 (D.C. Cir. 1971).

[49] International Harvester Company v. Ruckelshaus, 478 F.2d 615 (D.C. Cir. 1973).

[50] Chemehuevi Tribe of Indians v. Federal Power Commission, No. 71–2012 (D.C. Cir. Nov. 9, 1973).

[51] Mobil Oil Corporation v. Federal Power Commission, 483 F.2d 1238 (D.C. Cir. 1973).

and rate making as instruments of allocation, the one in response to claims that the agency must license in a sphere in which it has declined to do so thus far and the other in response to claims the agency could not legally set rates in a realm in which it has already done so.

Guidelines to Information Access: EPA *v.* Mink[52]

Following news in July, 1971, that the "latest recommendations" submitted to the president on the Cannikin underground nuclear test scheduled for November were the product of "a departmental under-secretary committee named to investigate the controversy,"[53] Congress-woman Patsy Mink urgently requested the president to release im-mediately the recommendations and reports of the interdepartmental committee. The request was denied, and Ms. Mink then filed an action under the Freedom of Information Act[54] to compel disclosure. She was joined in this by thirty-two other members of the House of Representa-tives. In all, nine documents were sought, including the report of the undersecretary's committee, a transcript of an oral briefing given to that committee by the Atomic Energy Commission, letters from the Environ-mental Protection Agency, the Council for Environmental Quality, and the Office of Science and Technology, and a report from the Defense Program Review Committee.

Under the Freedom of Information Act, the following matters are exempt from the requirement that government agencies shall make their information available to the public: those "specifically required by Executive order to be kept secret in the interest of the national defense or foreign policy";[55] "inter-agency memorandums or letters which would not be available by law to a party other than an agency in litigation with the agency."[56] Objection to disclosure of the requested information was based on these exemptions, agency counsel claiming that the documents were classified Secret and Top Secret pursuant to Executive

[52] *Supra*, n. 45.
[53] *Id.*, at 75.
[54] 5 U.S.C. §552 (1966). A separate action was brought to enjoin the test itself. Committee for Nuclear Responsibility v. Seaborg, 463 F.2d 783 (D.C. Cir. 1971). After adverse decisions below, plaintiffs appealed to the Supreme Court for an injunction. On November 6, 1971, the Supreme Court denied the applica-tion, Committee for Nuclear Responsibility v. Schlesinger, 404 U.S. 917 (1971), and the test was conducted that same day.
[55] *Id.*, at (b)(1).
[56] *Id.*, at (b)(5).

Order 10501[57] and that "they were prepared and used solely for transmittal to the President as advice and recommendations. . . ."[58] The federal district court agreed with the position of the resisting agencies, but the court of appeals reversed on the ground that the Freedom of Information Act did not sanction sweeping withholdings of information. The court instructed the district court judge to examine the classified documents to determine if the nonsecret components were separable from the secret remainder and able to be read separately without distortion of meaning through examination of the documents *in camera*. The district judge was also to decide whether "factual data" from the documents could be distilled out and made public "without impinging on the policy-making decisional processes intended to be protected" by the exemptions to the disclosure requirement.[59]

The Supreme Court reversed the court of appeals by a 5–3 vote (Rehnquist not participating), and Justice White, writing for the majority, proceeded to spell out definitive, albeit complex, views on the criteria to be applied by the judiciary in deciding on public access to withheld information.

Recognizing that the act was "broadly conceived" to permit access to information "long shielded unnecessarily from public view" and that it placed the burden of proof on the agency to justify its withholding action, White maintained that the conflicting claims over the documents must be considered in "the context of the Act's attempt to provide a workable formula that balances and protects all interests."[60] Insofar as the claim of secrecy was concerned, he rejected as "wholly untenable" any claim that the act subjected "the soundness of executive security classifications to judicial review at the insistence of any objecting citizen."[61] Neither could the act be construed in his view to authorize *in camera* inspection of a contested document bearing a single Secret or Top Secret classification. The district court could not consequently take on the role of separating secret from supposedly nonsecret matter and ordering the latter's disclosure.

White pointed out that the secrecy classifications of the documents and their characterizations as involving "highly sensitive matter that is vital to our national defense and foreign policy" were never disputed by

---

[57] 3 C.F.R. 280 (Jan. 1, 1970). As of June 1, 1972, Executive Order 10501 was superseded by Executive Order 11652, 37 Fed. Reg. 5209, which similarly provides for the classification of material "in the interest of the national defense or foreign relations."

[58] *Supra*, n. 45, at 76.   [59] *Id.*, at 78.   [60] *Id.*, at 80.   [61] *Id.*, at 84.

the plaintiffs.[62] In view of the classification and characterization of the documents and the ensuing failure to dispute them, the executive agencies "had met their burden of demonstrating that the documents were entitled to protection" under the secrecy exemption.[63]

Three of the documents were conceded by the agencies to be unclassified. With regard to these, disclosure was resisted on the ground that they were interagency memorandums used for the decision-making processes of the executive branch. White held that factual material not intertwined with policy-making processes could and should safely be disclosed. But he viewed the court of appeals remand to the district court as "unnecessarily rigid."[64] *In camera* inspection by the district court should not follow automatically from invocation of the act by a member of the public. Rather, "an agency should be given the opportunity, by means of detailed affidavits or oral testimony, to establish to the satisfaction of the district court that the documents sought fall clearly beyond the range of material that would be available to a private party in litigation with the agency."[65] For example, the agency could demonstrate by surrounding circumstances that particular documents contained no factual information separable from the advisory material. "In short, *in camera* inspection of all documents is not a necessary or inevitable tool in every case."[66]

To those interested in mechanisms for the allocation of common property resources, the message of the Supreme Court in the *Mink* case is a clear reminder that the Freedom of Information Act is no "open sesame" to obtaining agency papers and documents that bear on their programs or policies. Secrecy classifications must be disputed by those seeking papers so classified, and the Court's clear intimation is that the burden of proof in such situations is on the seekers. Where secrecy is not invoked, the agency may nonetheless resist submission of the materials to the district court for inspection. Lengthy and costly delays await the seeker of information if an agency elects to contest disclosure.

Douglas, in dissent, accused the majority of making a "shambles"[67] of Congress's objectives in passing the act; for "anyone who has ever been in the Executive Branch knows how convenient the 'top secret' or 'secret' stamp is, how easy it is to use and how it covers perhaps for decades the footprints of a nervous bureaucrat or a wary executive."[68] The majority's decision, in his view, enabled the executive to withhold

---

[62] *Id.*   [63] *Id.*   [64] *Id.*, at 92.   [65] *Id.*, at 93.   [66] *Id.*
[67] *Id.*, at 109.   [68] *Id.*, at 108.

information at will or whim and successfully to make secret "even the time of day."[69]

It must be recognized that the majority's opinion was based exclusively on statutory construction. It passed the ball—some might say the buck—to the people and their representatives. As Stewart said in concurring, Congress built into the Freedom of Information Act an exemption that provided no means to challenge an executive decision to stamp a document Secret "however cynical, myopic or even corrupt that decision might have been."[70] Since key governmental decisions that affect common property resources, such as this one on nuclear testing, are precisely the kind that "should be opened to the fullest possible disclosure," and since the reduction of the people and their representatives to a state of ignorance on such issues means that "the democratic process is paralyzed,"[71] the solution must lie with a further revision of the information statute that will genuinely protect the public's right to know. In any event, the Supreme Court emphasized through its ruling in *Mink* that it eschews the role of *deus ex machina*; to change what the majority views as the statute's plain meaning requires action by the people and their representatives.

Scope and Limits of Considerations of Environmental
Impact according to Judicial Constructions

Three recent cases typify judicial role in delineating the scope and limits of environmental considerations required of agency decision makers: *Citizens to Preserve Overton Park, Inc.* v. *Volpe*,[72] which involved provisions of the Department of Transportation Act of 1966 and of the Federal Highway Act of 1968; *Natural Resources Defense Council* v. *Morton*,[73] which involved relationships between the Interior Department and the National Environmental Policy Act; and *United States* v. *Students Challenging Regulatory Agency Procedures* (SCRAP),[74] which concerned the impact of NEPA on the Interstate Commerce Commission.

Overton Park dealt with the operational consequences of the prohibitions placed on the secretary of transportation by the Transportation Act and the Highway Act that prevented him from authorizing the use of federal funds for construction of highways through public parks if there is a "feasible and prudent" alternative route.[75] If no alternative

[69] *Id.*, at 110. [70] *Id.*, at 95. [71] *Id.*, at 94–95. [72] *Supra*, n. 46.
[73] 458 F.2d 827 (D.C. Cir. 1972). [74] *Supra*, n. 47.
[75] *Supra*, n. 46, at 405.

were available, the statutes allowed the secretary to finance construction through parks only if "all possible planning to minimize harm" to the park had preceded the authorization.[76]

In April, 1968, the secretary of transportation announced that he concurred with local officials in the belief that a six-lane interstate highway, I-40, should be built through a Memphis, Tennessee, public park which contained a zoo, municipal golf course, outdoor theater, nature trails, bridle path, picnic areas, and acres of forest. Twenty-six acres of the park would be destroyed by the proposed highway, and the zoo would be severed from the rest of the park. Final approval for financial authorization was announced in November, 1969. In neither his 1968 nor his 1969 action did the secretary issue factual findings or state why he believed there were no feasible alternative routes or why highway design changes could not be made to minimize shrinkage of the park area. Opponents of building the highway through the park had contended that it could feasibly be built to the north or south of the park; if it did have to go through the park, they argued it could be constructed below ground level, preserving the park's unity and contiguity.

The opponents got nowhere in the district court or the court of appeals. Their contentions that the secretary had violated the 1966 and 1968 statutes were summarily rejected. An 8–0 Supreme Court reversed the lower courts, however. Although the justices agreed with the lower courts that the secretary did not have to make formal findings regarding feasible alternative routes or planning to minimize harm, they felt, nonetheless, that the secretary had not shown that his actual choice was not arbitrary, capricious, an abuse of discretion, or otherwise not in accordance with law pursuant to the Administrative Procedure Act.[77] The justices then remanded the case to the district court for plenary review of the secretary's decision, the review to be based on "the full administrative record that was before the Secretary at the time he made his decision."[78] Justice Marshall, who wrote the Supreme Court opinion, authorized the district court to require administrative officials who participated in the decision to testify in explanation of their actions.

The Supreme Court did not seek to substitute its view of the desirability of construction of the highway for the secretary's; nor did it seek to impose intolerable burdens on his expertise and discretion. Rather, the Court sought to enhance public accountability by requiring that the

[76] *Id.*, at 405.   [77] *Id.*, at 416.   [78] *Id.*, at 420.

record be sufficiently detailed to warrant the conclusion by reasonable people that the decision was in accordance with the law.

The Court of Appeals for the District of Columbia Circuit faced a similar question concerning accountability for decisions by the secretary of the interior under the National Environmental Policy Act in *Natural Resources Defense Council* v. *Morton*.[79] After the district court had granted a preliminary injunction against the secretary's sale of leases to some eighty tracts of submerged lands for oil and gas development off the Louisiana coast, the secretary sought summary reversal. The court of appeals upheld the district court and ruled that "a sound construction of NEPA which takes into account both the legislative history and contemporaneous executive construction requires a presentation of the environmental risks incident to reasonable alternative courses of action."[80] The essence of the court's ruling was that NEPA requires not merely a detailed statement of alternatives, but also consideration and discussion, albeit succinct and pursuant to "a rule of reason,"[81] of environmental risks incident to each of the alternatives. "The subject of environmental impact is too important to relegate either to implication or to subsequent justification by counsel."[82] As in *Overton Park*, the judges here sought, not to invade administrative discretion, but to make accountability through review more feasible by insisting that the record show that "officials and agencies have taken the hard look at environmental consequences."[83]

Where the lower courts in *Overton Park* had rejected the protesters' claims and the Supreme Court had upheld them, the students in the *SCRAP*[84] case found their strongest support in the three-judge district court, which was then reversed in favor of the agency when the case reached the Supreme Court. The lower court had granted the students' request for an injunction prohibiting the Interstate Commerce Commission from permitting any railroads to collect a surcharge on freight rates, insofar as the surcharge affected goods transported for recycling. The ICC's orders had failed to include a detailed environmental impact statement as allegedly required by NEPA.

The Supreme Court reversed on the ground that NEPA was not intended to repeal by implication any other statute and that the Interstate Commerce Act had vested exclusive jurisdiction in the ICC over the suspension of rates pending final decision on their lawfulness. The basis

---

[79] *Supra*, n. 73. [80] *Id.*, at 834. [81] *Id.* [82] *Id.*, at 836.
[83] *Id.*, at 838. [84] *Supra*, n. 47.

for the Supreme Court's decision was a technical interpretation of the relationship between NEPA and the Interstate Commerce Act.[85]

Lest the decision be viewed exclusively as a negation of judicial concern with resource allocation, however, it should be stressed that this case was the most important one since the *Sierra Club* v. *Morton*[86] decision on the subject of standing. The Court's conclusion that SCRAP had standing to sue invigorates citizens' roles in assuring governmental accountability. The five law students who had organized SCRAP might have been declared without standing on the ground that they did not tangibly demonstrate any adverse affect on them by the ICC's action. Reiterating that aesthetic and environmental well being, like economic well being, are important ingredients of life in our society, the justices ruled that the students' claim of direct harm in their use of the natural resources of the Washington area was sufficient to meet the test of standing.[87] One might say that the judicial role in *SCRAP* was to encourage the monitoring of agency practices by citizen groups and the challenging of improper practices through the courts. The particular circumstances did not warrant injunction in this case; but far more significant than approval of the surcharge was the fact that the Court enhanced aesthetic considerations as components of standing and went on to consider the substantive issue of NEPA's impact on its merits.

Methodological Concerns of the Judiciary in
Reviewing Agency Actions

The court of appeals decision in *Calvert Cliffs Coordinating Committee, Inc.* v. *Atomic Energy Commission*,[88] which came a year earlier than its ruling in *Natural Resources Defense Council* v. *Morton*,[89] was especially noteworthy for establishing a sophisticated methodological framework for judicial review of agency allocative actions.

In holding the agency accountable to the courts for compliance with the substantive and procedural directives of NEPA, the court recognized that "these cases are only the beginning of what promises to become a flood of new litigation . . . seeking judicial assistance in protecting our natural environment."[90] Judge Wright's conception of judicial role was, explicitly, to make a reality of the promise of recent legislation to control "the destructive engine of material progress."[91] The duty of the judiciary was presented as "to see that important legislative purposes

---

[85] *Id.*, at 2417–22.   [86] 405 U.S. 727 (1972).   [87] *Supra*, n. 47, at 2415.
[88] *Supra*, n. 48.   [89] *Supra*, n. 73.   [90] *Id.*, at 1111.   [91] *Id.*

are not lost or misdirected in the vast hallways of the federal bureaucracy."[92]

That the duties assigned to the agencies in section 102 of the statute were qualified by the phrase "to the fullest extent possible" was not to be construed judicially as "an escape hatch for footdragging agencies."[93] The phrase did not make adherence to NEPA's requirements discretionary or turn the statute into a "paper tiger."[94] Wright proceeded to distinguish sharply between judicial reversal of agency actions for substantive reasons and reversal for failure to adhere to procedural standards. A substantive decision could not be reversed on its merits by the courts "unless it be shown that the actual balance of costs and benefits that was struck was arbitrary or clearly gave insufficient weight to environmental values."[95] But it was and is the responsibility of the courts to reverse an agency whenever the agency's decision "was reached procedurally without individualized consideration and balancing of environmental factors conducted fully and in good faith."[96]

To the agency's argument that the methodology required of it by the court's implementation of the statute would unduly restrict its discretion, Wright's response was that the court insisted on an adequate record demonstrating the exercise of expertise and discretion. Agency consideration of environmental factors must not be merely a "pro forma ritual";[97] the way to avoid ritualization is to examine the environmental costs and benefits of a particular proposal along with those of its alternatives. No doubt the court was limiting the agency's *procedural* discretion by forbidding it to bypass the weighing of costs, benefits, and alternatives; but it was enhancing *substantive* discretion by demanding its full exercise "at every important, appropriate and nonduplicative stage of an agency's proceedings."[98]

The central issue in *International Harvester* v. *Ruckelshaus*,[99] which also involved General Motors, Ford, and Chrysler, was the relationship between technological projections and actual test results in the EPA administrator's determination of whether to suspend for a year the 1975 emission standards prescribed by the Clean Air Act for light-duty vehicles. The administrator relied predominantly on his agency's projections in refusing the suspension, while the car manufacturers argued that actual test results were required to meet the administrator's burden of proof.

---

[92] *Id.*   [93] *Id.*, at 1114.   [94] *Id.*   [95] *Id.*, at 1115.   [96] *Id.*
[97] *Id.*, at 1128.   [98] *Id.*   [99] *Supra*, n. 49.

The court sided with the manufacturers insofar as it remanded the case to the agency for further proceedings. What was most significant about the case, however, was Judge Leventhal's probe of methodological considerations and of dimensions of expertise of the EPA and the National Academy of Sciences,[100] the latter body having been called on by the Clean Air Act to submit a semiannual report on technological feasibility.

Leventhal's review of substantive issues was far more precise than was the court's in *Calvert Cliffs*. Disagreement with his colleague over this extensive substantive review prompted Judge Bazelon to write a separate concurring opinion calling for remand to the agency on purely procedural grounds. An explanation for Leventhal's meticulous probe of substance here, however, could well have been the conflict he perceived between the National Academy of Sciences' conclusions about technological feasibility and the EPA's. The NAS conclusion was that technology was not available to meet the emission standards of 1975. Given "the knowledge and objectivity of that prestigious body"[101] and the reliance Congress placed on it to make an independent judgment, Leventhal did not believe it appropriate for EPA simply to revise the NAS assumption or alter its conclusion without demonstrating empirically through research and experience that EPA had knowledge superior to that of NAS. The substantive studies examined by Leventhal failed to show that EPA's knowledge was superior; thus, while Leventhal commended EPA for its "diligence" in undertaking a "prickly task,"[102] he ruled that the court could not affirm EPA's denial of suspension.

The nuance of language is important here, for nonaffirmation of denial of suspension does not mean "that the EPA's process must be brought to nullity."[103] The court declined to grant the manufacturers' request that it order a suspension, but remanded the case to EPA for further proceedings in which there would be "reasonable cross-examination"[104] as to submissions previously made as well as to new lines of testimony. What was necessary before the court would sanction the EPA action was a record of a "reasoned decision."[105] This means "in present context, a reasoned presentation of the reliability of a prediction, and methodology that is relied upon to overcome a conclusion, of lack of available technology, supported prima facisely by the only actual and observed data available, the manufacturers' testing."[106] The court's

---

[100] *Id.*, at 647–49.   [101] *Id.*, at 649.   [102] *Id.*, at 648.   [103] *Id.*, at 649.
[104] *Id.*   [105] *Id.*, at 648.   [106] *Id.*

message is clear even if its language is stilted: that an agency cannot rely on assumptions or predictions that are not somehow tied to empirical tests in deciding whether technology is available to meet statutory standards for clean air. Furthermore, when responsibility is assigned to another agency to report on technological availability and that agency's methodology and conclusions are not wholly consistent with those of the decision-making agency, courts will remand for further proceedings. They are not likely to choose between the conflicting methodologies and conclusions, but they are likely to demand further proceedings that can reconcile the dichotomies or lend palpable superiority to one over the other in the record.

Review of Agency Functions in Rate Making and Licensing as an Instrument in Allocation

Judicial oversight of administrative agency actions is often concerned with whether an agency may or must regulate facets of activity through rate making or licensing. At times agency action setting rates over products or items previously unregulated provokes a challenge; at other times the agency's refusal to regulate such a facet accounts for the claim that the agency is statutorily obliged to engage in licensing or rate making. *Mobil Oil* v. *Federal Power Commission*[107] is an example of the former and the *Chemehuevi Tribe of Indians et al.* v. *Federal Power Commission*[108] a prime example of the latter.

In *Mobil Oil*,[109] the FPC set minimum rates for the transportation of certain liquids and liquefiable hydrocarbons by natural gas pipeline owners. The court of appeals ruled that the FPC lacked jurisdiction to set rates for pipeline transportation of the liquid hydrocarbons and that the agency did not show, by substantial evidence on the whole record, that its procedures or findings with regard to rates for liquefiable hydrocarbons were adequate. Judge Wilkey recognized that, given the current technology for natural gas production, gas, liquid, and liquefiable hydrocarbons are often produced simultaneously from a single well. In the absence of facilities at each well to separate the three products for individual transportation, interstate gas pipeline companies at times transport them through a single pipeline.

The FPC, which has the statutory duty to establish "just and reasonable" rates for the transportation and sale of natural gas in inter-

[107] *Supra*, n. 51.   [108] *Supra*, n. 50.   [109] *Supra*, n. 51.

state commerce,[110] sought to assure that costs of transporting liquids and liquefiables were not passed along to gas consumers. After a fifteen-year period in which, on an individual basis, the FPC approved rate schedules on condition that the expenses be appropriately allocated among the three products, the agency adopted a sweeping general policy on allocation of costs and rates.

Stressing that "natural gas" means gaseous and not liquid petroleum, the court invalidated the commission's rate order for liquids as being beyond the jurisdiction granted by Congress. The only possible way the commission might have upheld its action would have been by demonstrating that "rate jurisdiction over liquids is necessary to preserve its rate jurisdiction over gas."[111]

With regard to liquefiables, the court held the agency's procedures defective. Although the court refused to require the agency to follow strictly the formal rule-making procedures of the Administrative Procedure Act, it concluded, citing its decision in *International Harvester*,[112] that neither do agencies have "carte blanche to proceed in any way they may see fit. Flexibility is not synonymous with uncontrolled discretion."[113]

Rate making rests upon findings of facts, and the facts must constitute substantial evidence in order to support the agency's conclusions. The court insisted that rate-making procedures "must provide some mechanism for interested parties to introduce adverse evidence and criticize evidence introduced by others."[114] This is necessary both to assure an accurate factual base for the agency's decision and to provide the reviewing court with a record from which it can determine whether the agency has properly exercised its discretion. The case was remanded to the commission for further proceedings.

In the *Chemehuevi Tribe*[115] case, the court had to decide whether fossil-fueled steam plants that obtained their waters from a major cooling system of the United States in a way affecting the river's navigability were subject to the licensing jurisdiction of the FPC. The Chemehuevi Tribe, who live on reservations along the Colorado River, claimed that they were threatened by air pollution from some of the plants in question and that they also had an interest in the quality and quantity of the river waters required to cool and condense the steam.

The FPC contended that it did not have authority to license such

[110] 15 U.S.C. §717d(a)(1938).   [111] *Supra*, n. 51, at 1249.
[112] *Supra*, n. 49.   [113] *Supra*, n. 51, at 1254.   [114] *Id.*, at 1258.
[115] *Supra*, n. 50.

plants, even though it would welcome congressional action confirming such authority. Petitioners contended that even if literal reading of ¶4(e) of the Federal Power Act[116] did not explicitly authorize licensing of steam plants, technological advances since the act was passed wrought such dramatic changes in the operation of steam plants that licensing was now essential to fulfillment of the purposes for which the FPC was established.

The court agreed with the commission. Although it recognized that the FPC might be the "logical agency to design and implement a national siting policy,"[117] the court declined to "accomplish by judicial fiat what Congress has refused or neglected to accomplish."[118] The court saw its role as "restricted to the statute as written by the Congress, illuminated by legislative history, and construed by the Supreme Court."[119]

Although the court denied petitioners' assertion that the agency had a general licensing power over steam plants, it ruled nonetheless that the commission did have jurisdiction to license the utilization of surplus water by thermoelectric generating plants of whatever sort. "At a minimum, Congress surely intended to give the FPC control over the use of surplus waters for the generation of power, no matter by what mechanical force the electricity is ultimately produced."[120] Judge Mc-Cree's 75-page opinion was an exhaustive probe of text and nuance of the statute, culminating in a decision that, if not identical with King Solomon's in suggesting division of the baby, satisfied both the court's obligation to be governed by the language of the statute and the desirability of nudging the agency toward a more affirmative and active role in this area of resource allocation. The net result once again was remand to the agency for further proceedings that would show on the record its utilization of its expertise.

CONCLUSION

This scanning of typical cases in which courts make and find law through constitutional and statutory construction and through monitoring the actions of administrative bodies evinces an aura of judicial thoroughness and integrity, but it does not produce uniform policies in the alloca-

[116] 16 U.S.C. §797(e)(1970). [117] *Supra*, n. 50, at 58. [118] *Id.*, at 60. [119] *Id.* [120] *Id.*, at 75.

tion of common property resources.[121] The courts have the skill and interest to monitor, supervise, and probe, and in general they welcome opportunities to exercise these functions. They do not, however, wish to be ideological forces skewing statutes to their own value preferences or imposing their beliefs upon agencies charged with decision-making responsibility. As we have seen, the most definitive assertions of role have centered on the essentials of process and methodology to be observed by decision makers. *How* allocative policies are made, more than their goodness or badness, is of primary judicial concern. Although the doorways to citizen participation in invocation of judicial roles have been narrowed by the limitation the Supreme Court has placed on class actions, the judiciary's current view of standing is sufficiently broad to assure substantial access by aggrieved persons.

The ultimate question is not whether one *can* sue, but whether one *should*. Those who see the judiciary in heroic images are doomed to enlightenment through failure; judges are not knights in shining armor or classical gods. For egregious miscarriages of justice where the legislative and executive branches offer no effective recourse, courts provide suitable, if not ideal, forums for redress. For challenges to agency actions, where procedures have been defective or substantive conclusions conflict with those of other responsible agencies, the courts also provide useful recourse. The usual results, however, are not substitutions of "right" for "wrong" decisions but rather remands to the particular agencies for further proceedings. Delay must invariably be a by-product of this judicial role.[122]

Given limited financial resources and my choice to allocate them to the quest for corrective policy action either via the legislature or via the judiciary,[123] I would choose the former.[124] My preference for and con-

---

[121] For a discussion of policy issues in the environmental field from a political science perspective, *see* Nagel, *An Epilogue on Unresolved Political Science Issues in Environmental Protection*, in THE POLITICS OF ENVIRONMENTAL POLICY (forthcoming).

[122] For a similar conclusion in the context of enforcement of private rights, *see supra*, n. 20.

[123] For a thorough discussion of preference for the legislature, as opposed to executive agencies, *see* HAEFELE, REPRESENTATIVE GOVERNMENT AND ENVIRONMENTAL MANAGEMENT (1973). Haefele argues that only in the legislature can the proper accommodation occur where there are as many competing interests as are involved in the allocation of resources. *Compare* Sive, *Some Thoughts of an Environmental Lawyer in the Wilderness of Administrative Law*, 70 COLUM. L. REV. 612 (1970). "How does the expertise of administrative agencies and courts compare in environmental cases? The writer submits that the bulk of the

fidence in legislative recourse would be attributable in large part, however, to the knowledge that the courts are available to me as ultimate protectors against abuse. There is additional comfort in the realization that agency officials and legislators are likely to be as aware of the courts' role capacity as I.

---

important questions in environmental cases call more for the talents and training of the courts and judges than for those of the administrative agencies and administrators." *Id.*, at 629. Those favoring comprehensive environmental planning also look to the legislature as the body best able to effectuate balancing. " . . . [T]he federal government must become the nation's comprehensive environmental planner. Washington must establish priorities for environmental protection, must calculate the 'tradeoffs' to be made between environmental protection and other national goals, and must plan resource use and protection over several generations." ROSENBAUM, THE POLITICS OF ENVIRONMENTAL CONCERN 152–53 (1973).

[124] Perhaps the most eloquent expression of the view preferring the judiciary to either the legislature or administrative agencies as means by which citizens can seek to protect their interests is SAX, DEFENDING THE ENVIRONMENT (1970). "Simply put, the fact is that the citizen does not need a bureaucratic middleman to identify, prosecute, and vindicate his interest in environmental quality. He is perfectly capable of fighting his own battles—if only he is given the tools with which to do the job . . . [T]he courtroom is an eminently suitable forum for the voicing of citizen concerns over the maintenance of environmental quality. The real virtues of environmental litigation have little to do with the common conception of niggling lawyers battling over the intricacies of some ambiguous words in an obscure statute. Rather, the availability of a judicial forum is a measure of the willingness of government to subject itself to challenge on the merits of decisions made by public officials; to accept the possibility that the ordinary citizen may have useful ideas to contribute to the effectuation of the public interest; and to submit to them if—in the rigorous process of fact gathering—those ideas are shown to have substantial merit."

JOHN HANSEN

Comment

I WISH TO COMMEND Rosenblum for his excellent paper and his perceptive views relative to the role of the courts in this interesting area. Had his paper been directed solely to a legal audience, I am sure most of the following comments would have been satisfactorily considered and resolved.

What legal meaning can be attached to the term *common property resources*? Rosenblum did not define what it was that the courts were supposed to be allocating and tended to treat the term as generally synonymous with the legally unspecific term *natural resources*. Since the term embodies two legal words of art, i.e., *common property*, I think that it would be revealing to explore the legal connotations of the term if for no other reason than to determine whether all the represented disciplines use it within the same frame of reference. I find that to exclude resources which are not the subject of property, first of all, and are not the subject of common property rights, secondly, is to exclude a great many of the resources considered in the papers presented at this conference, including Rosenblum's. Furthermore, it appears that our inability or failure to categorize certain resources, such as air and water, as common property resources in the legal sense is what governs our current approaches to their problems and causes us to adopt power-based regulatory approaches as opposed to property-based allocatory approaches. Though allocations do result from regulation of activities affecting resources, such as pollution, the legal focus is on the regulation aspect, not the resulting allocations. Thus, in dealing with resources other than publicly owned real property, a court (or legislature for that matter) may never conceive its role to be that of an allocator of a "common property resource."

The author is a Research Associate, Resources for the Future, Inc.

When a court acts as an interpreter or supervisor of legislative allocations, its role is really secondary. I believe Rosenblum fails to give adequate attention to the primary role of the courts as resource allocators in common law actions such as nuisance, trespass, and riparian rights. In such actions the standards to be applied are judicial standards, and the responsibility for the allocatory decision rests solely upon the courts and cannot be "blamed" or thrust back upon the legislature. In spite of the recent rash of legislative action in the resource field, the common law remains virtually intact as an independent source of rights and remedies. Curiously, it appears that no serious attempt has been made to integrate statutory and common law in this field.

Perhaps the reason that Rosenblum fails to develop this unique common law role of the courts is that his source of examples is largely limited to federal court cases, and federal courts are extremely limited in their ability to create and apply *federal* common law. Thus, examples of courts allocating resources according to judicial norms are to be found in state cases or in the few federal court cases where state common law is applied. Yet decisions like the *Bonelli* case, which he discussed at length, and *Illinois* v. *City of Milwaukee*, decided by the Supreme Court in 1972, evidence an interesting trend towards greater involvement of federal common law in the resource field. Although this will be welcomed by many, it should be recognized that federal entry into a regulatory field is usually followed by federal preemption of conflicting state regulatory activity and a resulting decrease in state initiative. If no preemption is intended, the result is likely to be that yet another body of law is superimposed upon this already crowded field, i.e., state common law, state statutory law, federal statutory law, and now federal common law. Moreover, if the *Bonelli* case is at all indicative of the common property resource prospects of federal common law, the outlook is not promising, for the result there was to "allocate" a common property resource into private property on the grounds that the state's interest therein was "limited" and that the state (public?) was not entitled to a windfall. It will be interesting to observe if the new federal common law of nuisance to be developed as a result of the *Illinois* case will result in a finding that Illinois's interest in the waters of Lake Michigan is similarly "limited" when weighed in the balance against Milwaukee's right to use the water and the economic effects of early abatement. Unlike the Holmesian approach in *Georgia* v. *Tennessee Copper Company*,[1] which accords federal recognition and

[1] 206 U.S. 230 (1907).

145

backing to a state's desire to be free of the effects of extraterritorial pollution, it appears that this is no longer a matter for determination solely by the plaintiff state but rather is merely one factor to be considered in the federal common law "balancing" process. For those of us who see greater benefits in state initiative than in uniformity of law, this diminution of the quasi-sovereign rights of states is not a good omen.

From an evolutionary standpoint, law involves the continuous search for identifiable substantive rights and the creation of correlative duties whereby such rights are preserved and protected. Environmental law is at an early stage in this process and is still groping for that ideal combination of legal relationships. Contrary to the belief expressed by professor Dorfman in this volume, there is no present citizen's right to clean water. In fact the existence and extent of a citizen's substantive right with respect to most of our common property resources are yet to be determined. In this regard it is important to distinguish between standing and substantive right, for the procedural legal interest recognized in *Sierra Club* v. *Morton*[2] and related cases is not one which will provide the basis for a suit for damages in the event of unlawful interference therewith. The common law affords a unique opportunity for determining substantive legal rights of citizens with respect to common property resources. The decision in any public nuisance suit involves a judicial allocation of the relative rights and duties of the plaintiff and defendant. Though the courts lack the ability to affect comprehensive allocatory schemes, they do have flexibility to tailor their decision so as to individualize the allocation to the particular circumstances involved in the suit. It is interesting to observe that the desire for comprehensive allocations such as have motivated the most recent Federal Water Pollution Control Act have not in fact resulted in comprehensive allocations of substantive legal rights to everyone. If one analyzes the FWPCA he finds that it provides for determination of only the substantive rights and duties of the dischargers in relation to the government. Apparently the allocation of relative rights and duties between dischargers and other users of the public waters is left to the courts for determination in accordance with judicial norms. Thus a discharger holding all the permits, authorizations, and certifications required by federal and state law may still be subjected to the imposition of more stringent duties as a result of a common law court action.

[2] 405 U.S. 727 (1972).

Though it is clear that present-day courts retain an important role in the allocation of common property resources, I strongly suspect that the judicial search for a substantive citizen's right will one day lead to the inquiry with which I commenced these comments. Attention will focus on the unequal allocations resulting from regulatory schemes and the constitutional implications of them. For some resources such as water, property concepts will be reconsidered and the long-dormant trust language in many state constitutions may be brought to life to justify new approaches to water pollution control which result in more equitable and/or efficient allocatory methods and possibly the imposition of duties on present-day users to preserve the resource for future generations. The prospects for an increasing role of the courts in these allocatory decisions are obvious.

J. CLARENCE DAVIES, 3d

How does the agenda get set?

THIS IS a preliminary status report on the early stages of a research project. The project is scheduled to last two years; I have been working on it about five months. Its purpose is to develop and test hypotheses to explain the process by which problems become political issues at the national level in the United States. Put another way, I want to be able to describe, in terms as rigorous as possible, how policy problems get on the agenda of the federal government. To provide the raw material to develop and test my hypotheses I plan to conduct a series of case studies of environmental issues. I shall rely on the existing literature for studies of other types of issues, bearing in mind that the agenda-setting process for the governance of common property resources may well be different from the process which typifies other policy areas.

ORIGINS OF THE STUDY

My interest in the question of how issues are formed or how the agenda is set springs from several sources. I have been dealing with environmental policy problems for more than eight years, and throughout most of that time two questions have haunted both the students of environmental policy and the more thoughtful environmental activists and practitioners—how did environmental policy come so forcefully to public attention and will public interest in the issue decline as rapidly as it arose?

The activists and practitioners have dealt with these questions mostly by assertion. It is dangerous to speculate in public about the disappearance of one's base of support. Thus, the conclusion of the 1971 annual report of the Council on Environmental Quality noted that

The author is Research Associate, Resources for the Future, Inc.

149

"there are those who doubt that we will have the will and persistence, and who believe that concern with the environment is simply a passing fad. But the evidence is to the contrary . . . . The pursuit of environmental quality has become a firm national commitment."[1] In its 1973 annual report the council cited some votes on bond issues and the success of candidates endorsed by the League of Conservation Voters and concluded that "these and other examples underline the long-term commitment of the public to a quality environment."[2]

The academics who have written about environmental politics and the history of the environmental movement have inevitably been faced with explaining the sudden rise in interest which occurred around 1969 and 1970. The explanations offered have been, for the most part, vague and tentative. They have included such disparate factors as rising affluence, worsening pollution, the politicization of the scientific community, the negative impact of the Vietnam war and the positive impact of the civil rights movement, the fear and ecological awareness generated by nuclear fallout, and the publication of Rachel Carson's *Silent Spring* and Paul Ehrlich's *The Population Bomb*.[3] These explanations are offered outside of any general or systematic context and are clearly ex post facto rationalizations for what remains a puzzling phenomenon.

The political science literature provides meager assistance in understanding the rise of issues. In almost all studies, the focus on how public policy is made has been on decision making, with the question of how things get to the point of making a decision being either taken for granted or written off as "nonpolitical."[4] There is a large volume of works on public opinion, but how public opinion is related to the issues with which the polity chooses to concern itself remains unclear.

[1] U.S., Council on Environmental Quality, *Environmental Quality: The Second Annual Report of the Council on Environmental Quality*, August 1971, p. 265.
[2] U.S., Council on Environmental Quality, *Environmental Quality: The Fourth Annual Report of the Council on Environmental Quality*, September 1973, p. 251.
[3] See, for example, Walter A. Rosenbaum, *The Politics of Environmental Concern* (New York: Praeger Publishers, 1973), pp. 53–89; Lynton K. Caldwell, *Environment: A Challenge to Modern Society* (Garden City, N.Y.: Anchor Books, 1971), pp. 3–23; J. Clarence Davies, 3d, *The Politics of Pollution* (New York: Pegasus, 1970), pp. 21–24; Roderick Nash, *Wilderness and the American Mind*, rev. ed. (New Haven, Conn.: Yale University Press, 1967), pp. 251–52, 256–58. For a call for more research on the problem see *Environmental Quality and Social Behavior* (Washington: National Academy of Sciences, 1973), pp. 38–40.
[4] For a partial exception see Charles E. Lindblom, *The Policy-Making Process* (Englewood Cliffs, N.J.: Prentice-Hall, 1968), pp. 13–14.

Similarly, the many discussions of the role of interest groups shed only some light on how such groups contribute to the rise or fall of political issues. The one existing book-length study of the agenda-setting process merely serves to underline the paucity of knowledge possessed by the political science community.[5]

One of the reasons why issue formation has not been studied more extensively is the difficulty of grappling with a wide variety of disparate actors, influences, and subject areas. Jacques Ellul's comment about the study of technology is apropos: "Since the scientist must use the materials he has at hand; and since almost nothing is known about the relationship of man to the automobile, the telephone, or the radio, and absolutely nothing about the relationship of man to the *Apparat* or about the sociological effects of other aspects of technique, the scientist moves unconsciously toward the sphere of what is known scientifically, and tries to limit the whole question to that."[6]

Another reason for the relative absence of concern with issue formation has been the usually implicit bias which tends to assume that in a properly functioning democratic society all problems that are sources of public discontent will be considered by the government. The agenda will be set by the "invisible hand" of democracy. This assumption has been called into question by a few political scientists, and it is these doubters who have begun to consider the problems of agenda setting in the United States.[7] Although they have strong biases of their own, biases which I do not wholly share, they have at least raised directly the question of the political process whereby a problem becomes an issue.[8]

[5] Roger W. Cobb and Charles D. Elder, *Participation in American Politics: The Dynamics of Agenda-Building* (Boston: Allyn & Bacon, 1972).

[6] Jacques Ellul, *The Technological Society* (New York: Vintage Books, 1964), p. 17.

[7] The seminal article in this connection is Peter Bachrach and Morton S. Baratz, "Two Faces of Power," *American Political Science Review*, vol. 56, no. 4 (December 1962), pp. 947–52. This article, in turn, derives from certain insights contained in E. E. Schattschneider, *The Semi-Sovereign People* (New York: Holt, Rinehart & Winston, 1961). For the further development of this set of theories see Peter Bachrach and Morton S. Baratz, "Decisions and Nondecisions: An Analytical Framework," *American Political Science Review*, vol. 57, no. 3 (September 1963), pp. 632–42; Peter Bachrach, *The Theory of Democratic Elitism: A Critique* (Boston: Little, Brown & Co., 1967); and Peter Bachrach and Morton S. Baratz, *Power and Poverty* (New York: Oxford University Press, 1970).

[8] The major bias of the Bachrach-Baratz school is a belief that issues which are in the interest of the public in general and of lower-class groups in particular are systematically excluded from the political agenda.

The confluence of the activists' concern about the origin and durability of the environmental issue and the questions raised by a few political scientists within the discipline have given rise to the current study. I make no claim to being the first to bring these two sets of questions together. In fact, one of the first extended studies to derive from the questions within political science was a study of the air pollution issue at the local level.[9] But we still lack any systematic view of the process of agenda setting. To provide such a view is the goal of my study.

THE BASIC MODEL

To explore the political world one needs some kind of model, or framework, as a guide. Raw empiricism, the accumulation of miscellaneous facts, works no better in political science than in any other discipline. The case study approach is necessary to tie theories to reality, but case studies without an explicit framework serve only to conceal an implicit theory or framework from both the researcher and his audience.

The framework, or model, that I am currently using is an adaptation of the work of David Easton.[10] It involves essentially four dependent variables: wants, demands, issues, and agenda items. The agenda-setting process is viewed as consisting of three phases: the initiation phase, where wants are created and in turn give rise to demands; the diffusion phase, where demands are converted into issues; and the processing phase, where issues are converted into agenda items. Let me try to put a bit of flesh on these taxonomic bones by discussing each of the dependent variables in turn.

Wants

A want is a disparity between an individual's or a group's perception of an aspect of the physical or social world and the values which the group or individual holds about that aspect of the world. In simpler terms, it is the feeling that something is wrong.

The two basic components which create wants—perceptions and values—are interrelated. We pay attention to what we value and we

[9] Matthew A. Crenson, *The Unpolitics of Air Pollution* (Baltimore: The Johns Hopkins Press, 1972).
[10] See David Easton, *A Systems Analysis of Political Life* (New York: John Wiley & Sons, 1965).

152

shape what we perceive so that it is more congruent with our values.[11] Conversely, our values are influenced by our "existential base," by such factors as where we live and how much money we earn.[12] These inter-relationships have been important questions for political discussion at least since the days of Karl Marx.

Despite these interrelationships, we can also examine the two components separately, especially when dealing with reactions to phenomena in the physical world. Regardless of the values of the citizens of Santa Barbara, real oil did wash up on a real beach there and kill some real birds. Regardless of what we think of air pollution (or whether we think about it at all), real gases and particles are breathed in by real people and this produces real diseases. Thus we can talk about the "real" physical world, although in many cases our view of the world is dependent not only on our values but also on our scientific and technological ability to detect and understand it.

It is likely that issues, insofar as they derive from the real world, are due primarily to changes in that world rather than to dissatisfaction with a long-existing state of affairs. These changes are largely the result of the development and application of technology.[13] Thus the study of issue formation inevitably intersects with the study of technological change, although it should be emphasized that changes in values and perceptions are probably more important in giving birth to issues than are real-world changes.

The study of issue formation cannot totally incorporate the burgeoning literature on technology prediction, technology assessment, and technological change. But it can pinpoint those issues in which technological change is a significant factor, and the ways in which the change contributed to a problem becoming a political issue. It should

[11] There is a large literature of social psychology which deals with these interrelationships. For a discussion of them in the context of political opinions see Robert E. Lane and David O. Sears, *Public Opinion* (Englewood Cliffs, N.J.: Prentice-Hall, 1964), pp. 63–70 and *passim*.

[12] See, for example, Karl Mannheim, *Ideology and Utopia* (1936; reprint ed., New York: Harvest Books, n.d.); and Werner Stark, *The Sociology of Knowledge* (Glencoe, Ill.: The Free Press, 1958). The term *existential base* is borrowed from Robert E. Lane, *Political Ideology* (New York: The Free Press, 1965), p. 411.

[13] For brief examinations of a large number of issues arising from technological change in the United States see Midwest Research Institute, "Public Concern Over Technology—Case Histories of Unstructured Technology Assessments," interim report no. 2 (January 18, 1972) and interim report no. 3 (May 10, 1973) to the National Science Foundation.

also be possible to operationalize the condition of the real world as a determinant of issue formation by roughly measuring such factors as air pollution levels, acres of land strip mined, and so forth. My own current suspicion is that the correlation between changes in the physical world and the formation of issues is not high, in other words that a problem often does not become a political issue when it is at its worst.

If we turn to values, the other component in the creation of wants, we find we are dealing with a set of much more slippery variables. Overall culture is obviously a critical factor. Interpretation of scripture is not likely to become a burning issue, either literally or figuratively, in the post industrial society. But to adequately explain the dynamics of cultural change it would be necessary to assume the mantle of a Hegel or a Toynbee, a role for which I am neither intellectually nor temperamentally suited. With respect to cultural change, as with technological changes, I plan to trace the effects of such change on issue formation, but I shall not attempt to account for the dynamics of the cultural change itself.

In describing the value component involved in the creation of wants there are also a variety of sociological and psychological factors which must be considered. The status and role of the individual or group and the personalities of the individuals will be important determinants of their values.[14] Karl Deutsch has suggested that the degree of "social mobilization," or modernization, is also a major factor in want creation.[15] However, examination of this variable would require a cross-national comparative study which is beyond the scope of the present effort.

Both perceptions and values are highly dependent upon the information an individual receives. Our perceptions of the real world are often mediated through television and newspapers. Our values are also shaped by the wide variety of sources of information to which we are exposed. As Irving Fox has commented, "He who provides the information provides the framework within which wants are generated." Thus even the earliest stage of issue formation is linked to the other stages and

[14] For a review of some of the literature on psychological variables see Kenneth H. Craik, "Environmental Psychology," *Annual Review of Psychology*, vol. 24 (1973), pp. 403–22. The influence of sociological variables, such as status and role, in the rise of political movements and issues has been frequently noted. See, for example, Richard Hofstadter, *The Age of Reform* (New York: Vintage Books, 1960), pp. 135–66; and Daniel Bell, *The Radical Right* (Garden City, N.Y.: Doubleday & Co., 1963).

[15] Karl Deutsch, "Social Mobilization and Political Development," *American Political Science Review*, vol. 55, no. 3 (September 1961), pp. 493–514.

to other issues. The diffusion of an issue will be through the information media, and this diffusion will result in the creation of similar wants among additional people. Also, the concern of information sources (including such sources as friends, neighbors, and fellow workers) with one issue may create related wants which give rise to additional issues.

It will be quite difficult to make the dependent variable, "wants," operational. Public opinion polls are probably the only direct source of information, but polls will be almost totally lacking for the early history of an issue. It is likely that the existence of a want will have to be inferred back from the existence of a demand. Despite this major difficulty, the concept of wants still seems useful as a way of delineating the roots of an issue and as a way of making clear that not all dissatisfactions result in demands placed upon the government.[16]

Demands

A demand is an expression of a want cast in terms that imply or state that the government should do something about the situation. The initiation phase of the agenda-setting process thus entails not only the creation of wants but the factors which lead individuals and groups to make the connection between their desires or dissatisfactions and the potential of government action to give relief or fulfillment.

Four types of variables are involved in explaining the transformation of wants into demands: political climate, participation, rewards or incentives, and the availability of routinized processes.

What I have termed the *political climate* ranges from the overall political culture to fluctuations in national mood. The political aspects of the overall culture are obviously important. For example, economic wants were usually not converted to demands in medieval Europe because they were not considered appropriate subjects of government action. On the other hand, family disputes, which would be of concern to the government of some tribal societies, are usually not considered appropriate demands in contemporary U.S. society.

The regime in power at any given time also influences the political

---

[16] In my discussion of wants I have avoided using the term *ideology*. Although ideology is inextricably related to the value component of want creation, the term has acquired such diffuse meanings that my current plan is to try to avoid its use as a major variable. For a review of the variety of meanings acquired by the term *ideology* see Willard A. Mullins, "On the Concept of Ideology in Political Science," *American Political Science Review*, vol. 66, no. 2 (June 1972), pp. 498–510.

climate and thus demand creation.[17] An authoritarian regime, for example, may succeed in suppressing dissent down to the point where some types of wants are no longer converted into demands. Even under the same regime, there may be fluctuations in national political mood which change the type and volume of demands. I suspect that wants were more readily converted to demands during the early years of the Kennedy Administration than during the later years of the Eisenhower Administration. As Joseph Kraft has said, "However difficult to measure, there is such a thing as a national mood, a climate of ideas that makes certain things acceptable—and others not."[18]

Variables related to political participation are perhaps the most influential factors in demand creation. These variables, which include status and role, individual psychology, and group memberships, have been extensively delineated by other researchers.[19] There are a large number of people who do not think of converting wants to demands because they do not participate in the political system in any meaningful way. They view government as such a distant and alien force that they do not think of it as a means for solving the problems of daily existence. That these nonparticipants are often the people with the greatest number of wants is a fact of considerable political significance.

For participants and nonparticipants alike, the rewards or incentives involved in making a demand will have an effect on whether a demand is made. A politician running for election will have a major incentive to convert wants into demands if he thinks that doing so will help him win the election. If the incentive is great enough, nonparticipants can be pushed into making demands. For example, Dan Gibson, an eighty-year-old coffinmaker who had lived all his life in rural Knott County, Kentucky, became a major actor in the fight against strip mining after

[17] I am using *regime* here in the sense it is used by David Apter to mean "concrete, standardized variations in arrangements and mechanisms of government" involving the links between government and elites. See David Apter, *Choice and the Politics of Allocation* (New Haven, Conn.: Yale University Press, 1971), pp. 130–31.

[18] As quoted by John C. Maloney and Lynn Slovonsky, "The Pollution Issue: A Survey of Editorial Judgments," in *The Politics of Ecosuicide*, edited by Leslie L. Roos, Jr. (New York: Holt, Rinehart & Winston, 1971), p. 78.

[19] See Robert E. Lane, *Political Life: Why and How People Get Involved in Politics* (New York: The Free Press, 1965); Lester W. Milbrath, *Political Participation* (Chicago: Rand McNally & Co., 1965); and Sidney Verba and Norman H. Nie, *Participation in America: Political Democracy and Social Equality* (New York: Harper & Row, 1972).

coal company bulldozers had threatened to destroy his family home-stead.[20]

Finally, the existence of some kinds of scheduled, routinized processes may facilitate the conversion of wants to demands. Development of a community master plan, highway planning, budget cycles, and elections all can serve as ways in which wants are reviewed and are converted into demands. The existence of such processes illustrates that demands can come from the top down, from the government itself, a point to which I shall return.

Although it may not be possible to determine exactly who or how many people are making demands about a given subject at a given time, there are ample ways to identify demands. Newspaper editorials, opinion polls, and statements by interest groups can indicate the existence of a demand.

Issues

An issue is a demand which has become politically significant because of the number or political influence of the people making the demand. The diffusion phase is a conversion of demands into issues as the demand becomes increasingly widespread or as it catches the attention of politically important individuals.

The difference between a demand and an issue is thus one of scope. A demand made by one lone individual is not likely to be an issue, although if that individual happens to be the president it probably is an issue. If one demand becomes one hundred million people making the demand, then it has become an issue. Because the distinction between a demand and an issue is one of degree, I plan to use a scale, or index, of "issueness" rather than try to arbitrarily classify a demand as an issue when it reaches some particular point.

Another difference is that wants and demands are felt and made by individuals. In the discussion above I have talked about wants and demands as characterizing either groups or individuals, but I have done this primarily to allow for the realities of the research which will probably necessitate inferring individual wants and demands from expressions made by groups. However, when we turn to issues, groups become the primary actors. This is not to deny the importance of key individuals but only to say that the definition of when something is an

[20] Harry M. Caudill, *My Land Is Dying* (New York: E. P. Dutton & Co., 1971), pp. 75–79.

issue will rely on the actions taken by groups. A demand becomes an issue when action is taken by the AFL-CIO or the *New York Times* or the Republican party or a state legislature, for example. It is groups that convert demands to issues.

The diffusion phase involves familiar phenomena. The interest groups adopt a demand, key individuals become interested, the mass media publicize those actions leading to further support, state legislatures may take action, and the opinions of the general public both influence and are influenced by these activities. New interest groups and new governmental institutions may come into existence as a result of the demands made. How and why these different actors relate to the issue-formation process raises a variety of intriguing questions. For example, do the media create issues or simply report on issues created by others? Under what circumstances does state action precede federal action, and under what circumstances does federal action come first? Does public opinion push interest groups into action or is the process the reverse?[21]

Many issues arise initially at the local level, and in these cases the diffusion process may involve an escalation to higher governmental levels. Because this study is focused on the national level, I do not plan to examine in depth issue formation within a locality. Although there are many similarities and parallels between issue formation at the local and the national level, there are also significant differences, and the intrinsic importance of national issue development is sufficient to warrant separate examination. However, because wants and demands are phenomena which characterize individuals, examination of these variables will presumably be equally applicable to all governmental levels. It is in the diffusion phase that the national focus becomes important.

As a demand becomes diffused among different groups and thereby converted into an issue, it may undergo change, and new demands or issues may be created. Radical student groups adopted environmental demands in the context of other demands for a drastic change in the regime, but this was not what motivated Richard Nixon to include environmental demands in his 1970 State of the Union Message. The

[21] Such questions have been dealt with extensively in the literature, although not in the context of issue formation. For a good summary see V. O. Key, Jr., *Public Opinion and American Democracy* (New York: Alfred A. Knopf, 1961). Also see Cobb and Elder, *Participation in American Politics.* I have dealt with the diffusion process and the creation of ad hoc groups at the local level in an earlier work. See J. Clarence Davies, 3d, *Neighborhood Groups and Urban Renewal* (New York: Columbia University Press, 1966), pp. 168–204.

Audubon Society's support for environmental legislation was activated by still another set of motives. Can we say that the radical students, Nixon, and the Audubon Society are adopting the same demands? I think we can, but the interaction among different demands and issues poses obvious research problems.

Agenda Items

An agenda item is an issue which is under active and serious consideration by the government.[22] Thus the processing phase involves the processing of an issue by the government, an acceptance by the government that action should be taken, or at least seriously considered, to deal with the issue. Government here can mean any of the three branches of the federal government, although this study will generally be limited to items on the presidential or congressional agenda. The operational definition of an agenda item would include the holding of a congressional hearing on an issue or inclusion of an issue in the president's legislative program.

The success of an issue in becoming an agenda item will depend on how it is viewed by the government. This will involve such factors as the political strength behind the issue (how much support it has), the cost of taking action (what resources would be required), precedents for taking action (are only incremental actions needed?), the extent to which other issues are competing for the government's attention, and the extent to which other issues or other demands within the government complement or are able to be met by action on the issue in question. Whereas the perceived receptivity of the government to an issue is an important factor in the conversion of demands to issues, it is the actual receptivity of the government that determines whether an issue will be converted to an agenda item.

What I have done so far is to sketch the outlines of a basic model of agenda setting, or issue formation. I have defined the major dependent variables (wants, demands, issues, and agenda items) and noted what seem to me to be the most important independent variables. The independent variables are a rather mixed "apples and oranges" collection. This is troublesome from the standpoint of neatness and simplicity,

---

[22] My use of the term *agenda item* corresponds roughly to what Cobb and Elder call an *institutional agenda item*. What I call an *issue* they would term a *systemic agenda item*. See Cobb and Elder, *Participation in American Politics*, pp. 14, 85–89.

but I suspect it is inherent in the complexity of the phenomena I am studying.

I have said almost nothing about the relative strength of the independent variables because the data on this will have to come from the case studies. I have also not said much about the dynamics of the model, how the variables interrelate with each other over time, because this also will depend on what the case studies show. However, a dynamic element is present in the model because of what might be called "cascading variables." I begin with wants as the dependent variable, but wants become an independent variable in explaining demands. Similarly, demands are an independent variable in explaining issues, and issues are an independent variable in explaining agenda items.

SOME PROBLEMS AND MODIFICATIONS

The basic model described here leaves some important questions unanswered. A brief examination of these questions and some resulting modifications in the model will provide further insight into the research I am undertaking.

Types of Issues

The tendency both in common parlance and in the political science literature has been to use the term *issues* as if it described a homogeneous set of things. But clearly there are a very large number of characteristics that can be used to discriminate among different types of issues. Which characteristics are used in studying the agenda-setting process is crucial because a mistaken choice could lead to very mistaken conclusions. The type of proposal, or issue, is probably very important in determining the nature of the process by which it becomes (or fails to become) an agenda item. In short, the type of issue is an important independent variable in the issue-formation or agenda-setting process.

In my research design I have made some choices concerning type of issue. I am studying *national* issues, as against state or local issues. My case studies will deal with *environmental* issues, although I hope to be able to use the secondary literature to determine the degree to which the subject matter of the issues makes a difference in the process. The research will use the three-phase model to examine what I term "subject" issues and "policy" issues and perhaps will also cover some "project" issues.

160

This last set of distinctions illustrates the importance of the choices about issue types. Subject issues are about relatively broad subjects such as air pollution, occupational health, or foreign trade. Thus we can pose the question, How did air pollution get to be an issue? Policy issues deal with specific policy proposals—the Clean Air Act, the Occupational Safety and Health Act, or proposed regulations to implement these acts. Project issues relate to policies which are specific to a particular locality or project, as opposed to policy issues, which are national in scope and effect. These distinctions would seem to be a matter of common sense and yet, as far as I am aware, they have not been made by other researchers. The failure to make the distinction can result, for example, in controversy about the importance of public opinion in issue formation, a controversy whose solution may lie in noting that public opinion is very important in the creation of subject issues but not very important in the creation of policy issues. Making the distinction also raises fruitful questions such as, How do subject issues become policy issues [or vice versa]? and, How is the form of policy proposals derived from general concern about a subject?

The literature does contain a variety of typologies for characterizing issues.[23] Environmental issues are sufficiently varied so that I hope to be able to determine, at least partially, which of the typologies are of maximum utility. But it must be kept in mind that the choice of issues to study will determine, at least to some degree, the results of the study, and therefore the typology used to describe the issues will also describe the applicability and generality of the results.

---

[23] For a useful summary of some of these typologies see Lewis A. Froman, Jr., "The Categorization of Policy Contents," in *Political Science and Public Policy*, edited by Austin Ranney (Chicago: Markham Publishing Co., 1968), pp. 41–52. The following sources contain proposed issue typologies: Theodore Lowi, "American Business, Public Policy, Case Studies, and Political Theory," *World Politics*, vol. 16 (1964), pp. 689–90; Cobb and Elder, *Participation in American Politics*, pp. 96–102; Apter, *Choice and Politics*, pp. 118–23; Murray Edelman, *The Symbolic Uses of Politics* (Urbana: University of Illinois Press, 1967), pp. 1–21, 155–56; Easton, *Systems Analysis*, pp. 142–43; Bernard Berelson and others, *Voting* (Chicago: University of Chicago Press, 1954), pp. 184–99; Lewis A. Froman, Jr., "An Analysis of Public Policies in Cities," *Journal of Politics*, vol. 29 (February 1967), pp. 94–108; Herbert J. Spiro, "Comparative Politics: A Comprehensive Approach," *American Political Science Review*, vol. 56, no. 3 (September 1962), p. 577. The theory of games has also given rise to a typology based on the pay-offs (zero sum versus nonzero sum, for example), number of players, etc. See William H. Riker, *The Theory of Political Coalitions* (New Haven, Conn.: Yale University Press, 1962).

Issue Change

Even after a choice of issues to study has been made, there may be major difficulties in defining the boundaries of what is being studied. At any stage in the agenda-setting process the content or context of a proposal may change so sharply as to call into question whether it is still the same proposal or issue. For example, in the initiation phase a single expression of a want may be converted into a variety of demands. The urban riots of the late 1960s were an expression of a want, but the demands into which the want was converted were very numerous and disparate.[24] The conversion of demands to issues can produce equally great changes as groups interpret demands to meet their own views and needs. Anyone who has followed the changes in a major legislative proposal can testify to the drastic changes in content that can take place during the processing phase.[25]

Interrelationship of Issues

One of the factors that will cause an issue to change in content is its relationship to other issues. In the example of environmental quality noted above, the environmental issue was related to the issue of radical change in the regime by some student groups, to the issue of divisiveness in the public by President Nixon, and to the issue of saving birds by the Audubon Society.

Aside from changing the content of issues, the interrelationship of issues can pose problems in explaining the way wants become issues. Can we explain how air pollution became an issue without explaining how the environment in general became an issue? Can we explain how the Clean Air Act Amendments of 1970 became an issue without explaining how air pollution in general became an issue? And, to complete the circle, can we explain how environmental quality became an issue without dealing with how its various components, such as air pollution, became an issue? The answer to each of these questions is almost certainly "No," and thus each issue must be examined in the context of its relationship to other issues.

[24] See Lindblom, *Policy-Making Process*, p. 13.
[25] For a good example see Daniel Patrick Moynihan, *The Politics of a Guaranteed Income* (New York: Vintage Books, 1973).

An Issue Interaction Model

The problems of issue change and the interrelationship of issues are closely tied because one of the major factors that determines how an issue changes will be its relationship to other ongoing controversies. Schattschneider illuminates one aspect of this connection when he states: "Why do some conflicts become dominant while others attract no support? Dominance is related to intensity and visibility, the capacity to blot out other issues. It is related also to the fact that some issues are able to relate themselves easily to clusters of parallel cleavages in the same general dimension. . . . Success depends also on the degree of dissatisfaction with the old alignment already in existence.[26]

The basic model discussed in the first part of this paper assumes that "the issue" can be readily identified. It may be necessary to develop a "macro" model which deals with the overall development and changes in an issue as a supplement to the "micro" basic model. As an example of the type of hypotheses that would be encompassed in the macro model, it could be argued that certain types of issues tend to expand to the outer limits of the real-world system with which they deal. A concern with poverty in Appalachia is converted to a concern with structural unemployment throughout the nation, and this in turn is translated into the issue of all forms of poverty in the United States. Concern with civil rights for blacks in the South is eventually translated into an issue of all minority groups in the country. Air pollution becomes an issue because there is already concern about water pollution, and in turn the air and water pollution issues become part of a larger issue which encompasses many aspects of man's relationship to nature. The dynamics of this process include the real obstacles to solving one problem without dealing with the others; the sensitization of the media and interest groups to a set of problems; and the search of bureaucratic institutions for expanded power that can be built on an existing base.

Nonissues

If one is to study how something does become an issue, it is obviously desirable to also study things that do not become issues. The study of nonissues poses almost insuperable research problems, and the difficulty of examining "nonevents" has been one of the major

[26] Schattschneider, *Semi-Sovereign People*, pp. 74–75.

criticisms leveled at those political scientists who have raised questions about how the agenda is set.[27]

It may be possible to study a few nonissues directly, such as fluoridation at the national level or selected public works projects that did not become controversial. However, the primary way in which my research will deal with nonissues is by describing and explaining the long time-lag that often intervened between a want or demand and the development of an issue, or by explaining the process whereby an issue that reached the agenda was then dropped from it. While such explanations may not account for all the reasons why certain subjects do not become issues, they should shed considerable light on the topic.

Government Initiation

The implicit assumption behind the basic model is that issues are generated somewhere in the general public and work their way up, through interest groups and the media, to the government. However, there is ample evidence that many issues are initiated from within the government. Lindblom notes that, "Policy makers are not faced with a given problem. Instead they have to identify and formulate their problem."[28] Bauer and his colleagues, in a classic study of the foreign trade issue, state, "A congressman needs issues in the public eye. He needs people who want favors from him. His stock in trade is his power to take action on things citizens care about. If there were no clamorous demands giving him the opportunity to show his worth, he would have to create them. And that, indeed, is what he habitually does. . . . Congress, second only to the President, is, rather, the major institution for initiating and creating political issues and projecting them into a national civic debate."[29]

Is the basic model applicable to cases where the initiative for the issue comes from within the government? I believe it is, although it may resemble a two-step process because the diffusion and processing phases will be closely intertwined. How the process works within the government—for example, under what conditions Congress, as against

[27] See Nelson Polsby, *Community Power and Political Theory* (New Haven, Conn.: Yale University Press, 1963). For an example of an attempt to study a subject-matter nonissue at the local level see Crenson, *Unpolitics of Air Pollution*.

[28] Lindblom, *Policy-Making Process*, p. 13.

[29] Raymond A. Bauer, Ithiel de Sola Pool, and Lewis Anthony Dexter, *American Business and Public Policy: The Politics of Foreign Trade* (New York: Atherton Press, 1964), p. 478.

the Executive, will be the initiator of an issue—will be a major focus of the study.[30]

Unpredictability

If the hypotheses developed in the study are to have maximum value, they should be capable of predicting what will happen in future cases of a similar type. But the study encompasses a variety of factors that seem to be inherently unpredictable. We do not understand much about the macroevents that can change the entire setting in which issues are formed. We could not predict the occurrence of the Russian Revolution, much less the Industrial Revolution. At the other extreme, issues have been greatly influenced by singular individuals, but whether we are talking about John Brown or John Muir or John Gardner, we are hard-put to predict either their existence or their effect. In the environmental area, issues have often been shaped by unpredictable events in the real world—temperature inversions, oil spills, floods.

Although the occurrence of these individuals or events may be inherently unpredictable, the setting in which they occur is crucial. How-much influence would a John Brown have in 1970? How much impact would a temperature inversion have had on the public mind in 1870? Natural disasters, charismatic individuals, and probably also dramatic documents (such as *Silent Spring* or *Unsafe at Any Speed*) can have a crystallizing effect, comparable to the effect of dropping a crystal into a supersaturated solution.[31] We may not be able to predict the occurrence of the crystal, but I hope to be able to describe the nature of the solution or setting, and thus, by delineating the actual process of issue formation I hope to be able to narrow down the range of the unpredictable and to put the impact of unexpected events and individuals into some kind of context.

THE CASE OF STRIP MINING

I can perhaps clarify the framework to be used in the study by briefly sketching how it would apply to a particular case. I have chosen the subject issue of strip mining as an illustrative example because it is a relatively well delineated issue and because it seemed to come closer

---

[30] An early study that focused on this question is Lawrence H. Chamberlain, *The President, Congress and Legislation* (New York: Columbia University Press, 1946).

[31] I am indebted to Marion Clawson for this analogy.

to the basic model than other environmental issues with which I was familiar. I have not completed my research on the strip-mining issue, and thus I use it here simply to show how the model might be applied.

Initiation Phase

If the origins of the strip-mining problem can be traced to one person, it probably would be an American inventor named William S. Otis. In 1839 Otis invented the steam shovel, a device which made possible large-scale removal of coal by stripping off the overlying land. A few years later, Otis was killed by one of his own inventions, an event that some might interpret as a portent of things to come.[32]

The steam shovel was not invented for the purpose of coal mining, and some years passed before it was applied for this use. Coal stripping on a minor scale had been practiced in the United States since the early nineteenth century, and in 1866 a comparatively large strip mine was opened at Danville, Illinois.[33] However, the amount of land disturbed by these operations was limited both by the crude methods used (the overburden, the land lying on top of the coal, was removed by horse-drawn plows and scrapers and hauled away in wheelbarrows and carts) and by the seasonal nature of the work (the stripping was done in the summer and the coal taken out in the winter).[34] In 1877 near Pittsburgh, Kansas, the steam shovel was first applied to coal mining, and the era of modern stripping had begun.[35]

The increase in the amount of land stripped in the last one hundred years can be traced largely to steady improvements in Otis's original invention. The size of the "dipper," the amount of earth that can be dug by a single scoop of a power shovel, increased from less than 1 cubic yard on the 1877 machine to 2 yards in 1904; 3½ yards in 1911; 6 yards in 1916; 12 yards in 1928; 30 yards in 1935; 60 yards in 1956; 115 yards in 1959; and 220 yards in 1969.[36] Thus the 1969 power shovel used in strip mining could dig up far more in a single scoop than the 1877 machine could in an entire day. Although the economic demand for coal fluctuated markedly, the amount of coal

[32] Robert F. Munn, *Strip Mining: An Annotated Bibliography* (Morgantown: West Virginia University Library, 1973), p. 9.

[33] "Strip Mining Builds for Accelerated Growth," *Coal Age*, vol. 71, no. 8 (August 1966), p. 113.

[34] John A. Hollingsworth, Jr., *History of Development of Strip Mining Machines* (South Milwaukee, Wis.: Bucyrus-Erie Corp., n.d.), p. 2.

[35] *Ibid.*

[36] *Ibid., passim;* Munn, *Strip Mining*, p. 10.

Tons (in millions)

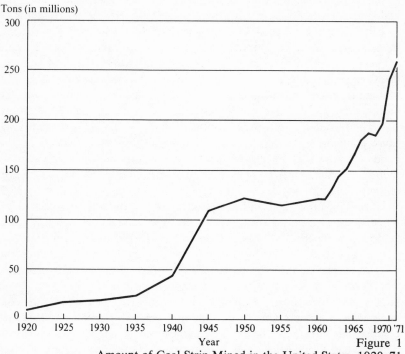

Year   Figure 1
Amount of Coal Strip Mined in the United States, 1920–71
Source: Computed from *Bituminous Coal Facts 1972* (Washington:
National Coal Association, 1972), pp. 52–53.

stripped each year grew fairly steadily and continues to grow (see figure 1).[37]

It did not take long for those living near strip-mined areas to conclude that there was a problem. Not only was the destruction of the

[37] Data on the amount of coal stripped annually are available from the U.S. Bureau of Mines. For annual figures from 1920 to 1971 see *Bituminous Coal Facts 1972* (Washington: National Coal Association, 1972), pp. 52–53. The best single measure of the problem would be the accumulated acres of unreclaimed strip mining. However, these data are not available. The Department of the Interior did produce an estimate of total accumulated acreage disturbed in 1964; see U.S., Department of the Interior, *Surface Mining and Our Environment*, 1967, p. 53. A study conducted by the department to update the 1967 report should be published in the spring of 1974. However, the 1974 figures are not completely comparable to the 1967 figures and are based largely on information provided by the coal industry.

167

land obvious, but the mining occurred largely in a region of the country, Appalachia, where the inhabitants had a strong attachment to the land and depended upon it for their livelihood.[38] In 1914 some residents of Indiana concluded that strip mining is "against public policy and community welfare . . . hundreds of acres of fine farming land are made unfit for future cultivation and destroyed as a substantial source of taxation."[39] Two years later *Coal Age* magazine reported that "the sentiment has developed in eastern Ohio against stripping, on the ground that it will leave the territory in a scarred, unsightly condition. . . . The business men's organization of Steubenville has passed resolutions condemning stripping, and the matter has been placed in the hands of attorneys to see whether grounds for an injunction can be found."[40] Thus wants were converted to demands early in the history of strip mining.

Loss of farming land and aesthetics were not the only impacts which aroused concern about stripping. In the Appalachian states many small landowners in the late nineteenth and early twentieth centuries had signed so-called "broad-form deeds" which gave coal companies the right to extract minerals from under the surface of the owner's property. The deeds were signed at a time when stripping was a rarely used and largely unknown form of mineral extraction. In later years the coal companies thus were able to strip mine a person's property and pay no compensation because the owner, or more likely his parents or grandparents, had deeded the rights to extract the coal. Thus numerous small property owners were severely and directly affected by the increasing strip mining of coal.

Diffusion Phase

Local demands to control the abuses of strip mining eventually led to the passage of state legislation. West Virginia was the first state to pass a strip-mining law in 1939.[41] In the same year a bill to compel strip-mine operators to level off and replace soil turned in mining was

---

[38] See Harry M. Caudill, *Night Comes to the Cumberlands* (Boston: Little, Brown & Co., 1962).

[39] "Opposition to Stripping in Indiana," *Coal Age* (December 12, 1914), p. 965, quoted in Munn, *Strip Mining*, p. 30.

[40] "Mining with Electric Shovels," *Coal Age* (March 25, 1916), p. 533, quoted in Munn, *Strip Mining*, p. 30.

[41] U.S., Department of the Interior, *Surface Mining*, p. 74.

defeated in the Illinois legislature.[42] In 1941 Indiana passed a law requiring reclamation of strip-mined land. Illinois followed suit in 1943, Pennsylvania in 1945, Ohio in 1947, Maryland in 1955, and Kentucky in 1964.[43]

The forces that gave rise to the state legislation are not yet clear. In Pennsylvania it seems to have been the local fishing and game clubs who were most influential in getting the state legislature to act.[44] The 1964 Kentucky law was sponsored by the Kentucky Farm Bureau Federation and the State Association of Soil Conservation Districts. It was supported by the League of Kentucky Sportsmen, the Kentucky League of Women Voters, and the Garden Clubs of Kentucky.[45] The motivation of these groups was probably varied. For the fishermen, strip mining presented a real threat because acid mine drainage from the stripping killed the fish in the streams. (Acid mine drainage also comes from underground mines, but the acid drainage from surface mines is more severe.) For the farmers, stripping was viewed as the destruction of agricultural land, a symbolically offensive action even if the economic consequences were minimal. For all these groups, the aesthetic blight caused by stripping probably provided a major motivation for action.

In any case, state action was clearly one of the factors which contributed to a demand for national action. The state laws were generally ineffective, thus forcing those favoring controls to turn to Washington.[46] Also, in some cases state officials seem to have encouraged the state's congressional delegation to push for national action, perhaps motivated by recognition of their own ineffectiveness or by fear of the competitive disadvantages which might result from stringent regulation within only one or two states.[47] For example, the Kentucky Strip Mining and Reclamation Commission, in a 1965 report, noted that "the present

[42] "Kill Illinois Strip-Mine Bill," *Coal Age* (June 1939), p. 85, quoted in Munn, *Strip Mining*, p. 21.
[43] U.S., Department of the Interior, *Surface Mining*, pp. 74, 99; and U.S., Department of the Interior, *Study of Strip and Surface Mining in Appalachia: An Interim Report to the Appalachian Regional Commission*, June 30, 1966, pp. 31–33.
[44] Interview no. 6. (I have footnoted interviews by number to preserve the anonymity of informants without losing track of the source of the information.)
[45] Kentucky, Department of Natural Resources, The Strip Mining and Reclamation Commission, *Strip Mining in Kentucky*, 1965, p. 27.
[46] U.S., Department of the Interior, *Study of Strip and Surface Mining*, p. 4.
[47] Interview no. 6.

relationship, of regulating to non-regulating states, makes for relatively greater coal production in the lower-cost, non-regulated state. Imposition of uniform controls would increase production in states now regulated, relative to presently non-regulated states, other things equal."[48]

A second factor in the diffusion process was the emergence of a national anti-strip-mining spokesman in the person of Harry Caudill, a Kentucky lawyer.[49] Caudill's actions, speeches, and writings brought the strip-mining problem to a national audience. In 1962 he published an article in the *Atlantic Monthly* entitled "The Rape of the Appalachians,"[50] and in the same year his book on the Cumberlands, which contained a sharp attack on strip mining, received wide circulation.[51] Caudill succeeded in providing the arguments, the images, and the heroes which gave fire to the antistripping forces.[52]

The mass media, particularly the *New York Times*, also brought national attention to strip mining. Ben Franklin, a reporter for the *Times,* actually participated in the struggle when he intervened, in 1965, with Governor Edward Breathitt of Kentucky to get the governor to meet with representatives of the Appalachian Group to Save the Land and People.[53] The Appalachian Group was one of several local or state groups formed to oppose stripping. However, these ad hoc groups did not concern themselves with action outside their particular state, and the national environmental groups do not seem to have entered the political picture until sometime in the mid-1960s.[54]

Another factor that was of crucial importance in the diffusion process was somewhat fortuitous. In 1960 John F. Kennedy was campaigning

[48] Kentucky, Department of Natural Resources, The Strip Mining and Reclamation Commission, *Strip Mining in Kentucky*, p. 27. It should be noted, however, that the commission's conclusion favored an interstate compact rather than federal intervention.

[49] See David G. McCullough, "The Lonely War of a Good Angry Man," *American Heritage*, vol. 21 (December 1969), pp. 97–113.

[50] *Atlantic Monthly*, vol. 209 (April 1962), pp. 37–42.

[51] Caudill, *Night Comes.*

[52] These are summarized in Caudill, *My Land Is Dying.* Caudill provides a good example of the function of the "mythmaker" in the issue-formation process. I use the term *myth* not to imply any lack of truth but rather in the sense of a set of symbols which provide emotional fervor to those concerned about an issue.

[53] *Ibid.*, pp. 78–79. I have not yet gone through the strip-mine articles in the *New York Times* to ascertain the timing or exact role of the newspaper's coverage.

[54] See Rosenbaum, *Politics of Environmental Concern*, pp. 216 ff.

for the Democratic presidential nomination. His success came to hinge on the West Virginia primary, and Kennedy spent a month campaigning in West Virginia. He resolved to do something about the poverty and other ills of the state, and his redemption of this pledge led to the processing phase of the strip-mine issue.[55]

Processing Phase

Kennedy's first response to the needs of Appalachia was the Area Redevelopment Act, which was signed into law May 1, 1961.[56] However, this act was not directed specifically at Appalachia, and the Conference of Appalachian Governors, which had been formally organized in 1961, considered its provisions inadequate to meet the needs of their area.[57]

In March, 1963, disastrous floods hit the Cumberlands. The damage caused by the floods and the dissatisfaction caused by two years of experience with the Area Redevelopment Act led the Appalachian governors to revive a proposal they had made two years earlier for the creation of an Appalachian Regional Commission. On April 9, 1963, Kennedy met with the governors and at the meeting announced the establishment of the President's Appalachian Regional Commission. The commission was a temporary joint federal-state group headed by Under Secretary of Commerce Franklin D. Roosevelt, Jr. Its job was to prepare a development plan for Appalachia and legislative proposals necessary to implement such a plan. The commission delivered its report to President Lyndon B. Johnson in April, 1964, and three weeks later the president submitted to Congress a bill carrying out most of the report's recommendations.[58]

The Appalachian bill, as submitted to Congress, called for the creation of a permanent Appalachian Regional Commission and for funds that could be used to reclaim strip-mined areas, but it contained no provisions to deal with the overall problem of strip mining. This was of particular concern to Representatives Joseph McDade and Daniel Flood

---

[55] On Kennedy and West Virginia see Theodore H. White, *The Making of the President 1960* (New York: Atheneum Publishers, 1961), pp. 101–14; and James L. Sundquist, *Politics and Policy: The Eisenhower, Kennedy, and Johnson Years* (Washington: The Brookings Institution, 1968), pp. 83–104. According to one informant, Kennedy talked to Caudill several times during the campaign (interview no. 4).

[56] See Sundquist, *Politics and Policy*, pp. 83–85.

[57] *Ibid.*, p. 101.

[58] *Ibid.*, pp. 101–3.

of Pennsylvania. The Pennsylvania congressmen had for a long time campaigned for action to deal with acid mine drainage, which was a major water pollution problem in western Pennsylvania and was one of the damaging consequences of both strip and underground mining. In 1955 McDade had succeeded in getting a federal law establishing a federal-state program to control the mine drainage problem,[59] but it was clear that more was needed. Thus McDade and Flood introduced an amendment to the Appalachian bill providing for a two-year study of the strip-mining problem and requiring that "the Secretary of the Interior shall submit to the President his recommendations for a long-range comprehensive program for reclamation and rehabilitation of strip and surface mining areas in the United States and for the policies under which the program should be conducted, and the President shall submit these to the Congress, together with his recommendations, no later than July 1, 1967."[60] Early in 1965 the Appalachian Regional Development Act, including the strip-mining study, passed the Congress and was signed into law.[61]

In 1966 the Interior Department submitted its interim study report to the Appalachian Regional Commission. The report stated that "the Appalachian States should establish laws and regulations that will provide sufficient authority to regulate strip and surface mining. . . . Should the individual states fail to provide adequate controls within a reasonable period of time, the Congress can be expected to take such steps as may be necessary to protect the public interest."[62] In its final report a year later the department had considerably strengthened this recommendation: "Federal standards and requirements should be developed for the reclamation and rehabilitation of surface mining areas."[63]

President Johnson sent the Interior report to Congress and said that he would submit specific legislation to implement its recommendations. However, given that it was late in the congressional session, it was decided to delay sending legislation until 1968. On March 8, 1968, the president, in his Message to Congress on Conservation, proposed adoption of the Surface Mining Reclamation Act of 1968, a bill which

[59] Act of July 15, 1955, as amended, 30 U.S.C. 571–6.
[60] The Appalachian Regional Development Act of 1965 (P.L. 89–4), §205(c).
[61] See Sundquist, *Politics and Policy*, pp. 103–5.
[62] U.S., Department of the Interior, *Study of Strip and Surface Mining*, p. 4.
[63] U.S., Department of the Interior, *Surface Mining*, p. 90.

he sent to the Hill with his message.[64] The bill was based largely on existing state legislation.[65]

In May, 1968, the Subcommittee on Minerals, Materials, and Fuels of the Senate Interior and Insular Affairs Committee held hearings on the administration bill and two other strip-mining bills.[66] The full committee took no action, and the House did not even hold hearings on the bill. This inaction was due primarily to strong opposition to the bill from the American Mining Congress and other industry groups. There was little support from conservation or other groups to offset the industry opposition.[67] Thus by mid-1968 strip mining was no longer an agenda item for the government.

When the Nixon Administration came to power in 1969, strip mining was not on its agenda. The subject was not mentioned in the president's 1970 Message on the Environment.[68] However, the diffusion process, both within and outside Congress, had accelerated. By 1970 the environmental movement was in full flower, and strip mining was a matter of active concern to groups such as the Sierra Club, the Wilderness Society, the Izaak Walton League, the Audubon Society, the Environmental Defense Fund, and the Natural Resources Defense Council. In 1971 these groups joined together to form the Coalition Against Strip Mining.[69] The states were also active. Arkansas, Minnesota, and North Dakota passed new laws to regulate strip mining, and a number of other states strengthened their existing laws.[70] Within Congress, more than a dozen bills were introduced calling for federal regulation of strip mining.

When the assistant secretaries within the Department of the Interior were requested to submit ideas for the 1971 administration legislative

[64] *Congress and the Nation* (Washington: Congressional Quarterly Service, 1969), vol. 2, p. 489.

[65] Interview no. 4.

[66] *Congress and the Nation*, vol. 2, p. 489. The three bills were S. 3132 (the administration bill), S. 3126, and S. 217.

[67] Interview no. 4.

[68] "Message on the Environment," February 10, 1970, reprinted in U.S., Council on Environmental Quality, *Environmental Quality: The First Annual Report of the Council on Environmental Quality*, 1970, pp. 254–71.

[69] Rosenbaum, *Politics of Environmental Concern*, p. 217.

[70] U.S., Congress, House, Committee on Interior and Insular Affairs, Subcommittee on the Environment and Subcommittee on Mines and Mining, *Regulation of Surface Mining: Hearings*, serial no. 93-11, 1973, part 2, pp. 1043, 1098–1105, 1625.

program, strip mining was notably absent from their suggestions. But Roger Williams, a geologist who had directed the staff which produced the 1967 Interior strip-mining report, was a special assistant to Interior Secretary Walter Hickel. Williams on his own initiative drafted an updated version of the 1968 bill. Hickel liked the idea and sent the bill forward to the White House.[71] The president's 1971 Environmental Message proposed "a Mined Area Protection Act to establish federal requirements and guidelines for state programs to regulate the environmental consequences of surface and underground mining."[72]

The House and Senate held hearings in 1971 on the administration and other strip-mining bills. Hearings continued in 1972, but the Ninety-second Congress was unable to reach agreement on a bill. The White House resubmitted a bill in 1973. In October, 1973, the Senate passed a bill to regulate strip mining, and action by the House is expected in 1974.

Conclusions

A few brief tentative conclusions can be drawn about the strip-mining case in the context of the agenda-setting process. These include the following:

• The development of the strip-mining issue conformed reasonably well to the outlines of the basic model. The issue began with local demands, was diffused through interest groups, the media, and state action, and finally became part of the national agenda through the interaction of Congress and the Executive.

• The diffusion phase of the issue continued after the issue became an agenda item. This is what enabled the issue to get back on the agenda a second time.

• The strip-mining problem resulted, to a great extent, from the application of new technology, specifically the steam shovel. One aspect of the application of this technology was that groups whose interests were originally compatible became antagonists because their interests became incompatible. This is most vividly illustrated by the current antagonism between landowners in Appalachia and the coal companies with respect to exercising the rights conveyed by broad-form deeds.

• The focus throughout the strip-mining issue has been on the

---

[71] Interview no. 4.

[72] *The President's 1971 Environmental Program*, March 1971, p. 18. See *ibid.*, pp. 271–88, for the text of the bill.

174

mining of coal, although coal accounts for only about 40 percent of the land strip mined in the United States. There are good, substantive reasons for this focus (other forms of stripping do not create an acid mine drainage problem, for example), but it has also been determined by the history of the problem and the political forces involved. As Haefele has said, how an issue is framed "determines not only which people are for it and which against . . . but also the intensities of feeling pro and con."[73]

• National interest groups, with the possible exception of the media, do not seem to have been important in originally getting the issue on the national agenda. They may have been more important in getting it back on the agenda in 1971.

• National groups representing industry do seem to have been important in getting the issue off the agenda in 1968. At least at certain stages of certain issues, political power exercised by a comparatively small group may be more effective in getting an issue off the agenda than in trying to prevent it from getting on the agenda in the first place.

• The media, specifically the *New York Times*, did play some role in bringing the issue to national attention. The role of the *Times* involved searching out a story rather than reacting to national events.

• Action by state legislatures and the resulting impact on the state congressional delegation seems to have been an important part of the agenda-setting process.

• At the federal level, Congress has been primarily responsible for calling attention to the problem. But only inclusion in the president's legislative program has given the issue enough push to put it on the congressional agenda.

• The political system has taken a long time to convert demands into an issue and an issue into an agenda item. This is a subjective judgment, but it will be interesting to compare the time consumed on strip mining with the time taken by other issues.

• It is very difficult to know how important key individuals were. How different would the history of the issue have been if it had lacked Caudill, Kennedy and the West Virginia primary, Roger Williams in the secretary of the interior's office? Perhaps not very different, but there is no sure way of telling.

[73] Edwin T. Haefele, *Representative Government and Environmental Management* (Baltimore: The Johns Hopkins University Press for Resources for the Future, Inc., 1973), p. 180.

175

THE IMPORTANCE OF THE AGENDA-SETTING PROCESS

Having outlined an approach to the issue-formation, or agenda-setting, process, the question must still be answered as to why it is an important process to study. Why is such a study worth undertaking?

The most fundamental answer is simply that issue formation is a basic part of the policy-making process. Thus an understanding of how the agenda is set should significantly improve our understanding of how policy is made.

The issue-formation process, however, transcends questions of how particular policies are made. How the agenda is set both reflects the structure of power in a society and is a key determinant of who has power. As Schattschneider has said, "Political conflict is not like an intercollegiate debate in which the opponents agree in advance on a definition of the issues. As a matter of fact, *the definition of the alternatives is the supreme instrument of power*; the antagonists can rarely agree on what the issues are because power is involved in the definition. He who determines what politics is about runs the country, because the definition of alternatives is the choice of conflicts, and the choice of conflicts allocates power."[74] Haefele makes the same point in the language of social choice theory: "Pollution may be regarded as a current problem of intense interest, but the way in which issues are formed about the problem will greatly affect the distribution of intensities of interest. . . . The man or group who is successful in forming the issue determines the relative . . . ranking that the problem will take, not only in his preference orderings *but also in everyone else's*."[75]

We can also look at issue formation as an information process. From the perspective of the government, the process provides the information necessary to maintain order. That is, it is the mechanism whereby government determines what demands of society must or should be met to keep the government in power and/or the society stable. From the perspective of groups within the society, issue formation is the mechanism by which they inform the government of their wants and demands and thus initiate the process of having their demands satisfied by the government. How the agenda is set is a key determinant of the stability of the society and a crucial indicator of how well the political process is functioning.

[74] Schattschneider, *Semi-Sovereign People*, p. 68 (italics his).
[75] Haefele, *Representative Government*, pp. 32–33 (italics his).

In examining agenda setting, I am dealing with what is probably the most important information process in the political system. The importance of this type of information both for the government and in other types of organizations has gained increasing recognition.[76] David Apter, for example, has recently published a theory which postulates an inverse relationship between information and coercion in any given political regime.[77] The examination of issue formation should provide a concrete application of the largely theoretical examination of the importance of information in the political system.

I doubt that my study will produce any specific proposals for improving the U.S. political system. It is not designed to do so. Rather, it is undertaken with the belief that improvements in the system are more likely to be successful if the system is understood. I hope that the study will contribute to such understanding.

[76] For its importance in government see Karl W. Deutsch, *The Nerves of Government* (1963; New York: The Free Press, 1966). For its importance to organizations in general see Kenneth J. Arrow, "Limits of Organization," mimeographed, Fels Discussion Paper No. 27 (Philadelphia: University of Pennsylvania, The Fels Center of Government, February 1973), chap. 3.

[77] Apter, *Choice and Politics.*

IRVING K. FOX

Comment

THE RESEARCH project outlined in this paper addresses an important set of issues concerned with the governance of common property resources. Furthermore, the model and concepts developed as a structure for the investigation provide a sound framework for pursuing the objectives Davies has in mind. Since the paper reflects such careful thought and such a thorough knowledge of the subject, it is difficult for me to raise suitable questions or offer worthwhile comment. My thoughts about the project are limited to its ambitious nature, the complexity of the processes that Davies proposes to unravel, and what these may imply for the strategy he pursues.

I wish to emphasize at the outset the importance I attach to a better understanding of the agenda-setting process. Davies has demonstrated that our understanding is very limited. There is evidence to indicate that important wants fail to receive the consideration they deserve in public decision-making processes. No matter how well a political process functions when an item gets on the agenda, the process is not serving the purpose intended if an item important to a substantial portion of the population never achieves active consideration. Until we understand much better than we now do the processes whereby wants eventually achieve active consideration, we will not appreciate the extent to which the political process is functioning effectively. Such knowledge must, of course, precede any effort to develop remedies for existing deficiences.

While recognizing the importance of the agenda-setting process, and granting the significance of environmental issues, it is essential to recognize that the task that Davies has set for himself is an especially

The author is Director, Westwater Research Centre, University of British Columbia.

complex one. This in part is attributable to the modest amount of work that has been done on this general subject, but the difficulty has been greatly increased because the emergence of environmental issues was so deeply interwoven with the complex political phenomena of the 1960s. These phenomena were associated with the Vietnam war and a range of disaffections with the functioning of U.S. society. The study of the agenda-setting process would be difficult for a relatively simple issue that had not become deeply interwoven with other issues. The difficulty is multiplied in the case of environmental issues.

Although this situation might lead one to wonder whether the study of agenda setting should begin with environmental issues, I assume that for a number of reasons the subject of research cannot be changed to a set of issues that would offer a simpler problem. On this assumption, it seems wise to give careful consideration to the strategy being perused in order to deal as effectively as practicable with the complex problem being addressed. This leads to the question of how the problem might be defined so as to produce the most valuable results with the resources available. It appears to me that there are two possibilities that might be considered, and no doubt Davies has given thought to each of these.

One possibility is to limit the range of issues that are addressed. Instead of trying to be comprehensive in dealing with the appearance of the environment on the agenda, the project might be limited, for example, to air and water pollution. Just how limited the coverage of the study should be is impossible for me to say, but I expect there would be merit in confining the investigation to two or three of the major environmental areas.

The other possibility for restricting scope of the study to make the investigation more manageable is to cover only a portion of the process from the emergence of wants to their appearance on the national agenda. Davies has, in effect, done this by indicating that because of the difficulty in dealing with wants, this stage of the agenda-setting process will receive little attention. While I agree with the need to circumscribe the scope of the study, I am disappointed to see this part of the process omitted from careful investigation.

If we are serious about the desirability of having governmental institutions that are responsive to individual preferences, the process by which wants are formed and get translated into demands becomes the most fundamental stage in agenda setting. This is so, I would suggest, for at least two major reasons. The most obvious one is that if

179

the legitimate wants of a substantial number of people never become articulated as demands to be considered through political processes, the democratic process is being frustrated. An equally important reason is that want formation has never been dealt with adequately in democratic theory.

Both economic theory and political theory assume that individuals have wants but say little or nothing about the influences that determine them. There is a widely held view—and no doubt a valid one—that the information an individual receives has an influence upon his preferences, but it is not entirely clear how great this influence is or what other conditions operate to make information an important influence. If information is, as suspected, an important determinant of want formation, those who generate and communicate information have an extremely important role in determining social preferences. This idea is an old one and underlies much of the current concern about the effects of advertising and the influence of the media. While it is an old idea, it won't go away, and it has important implications for democratic government.

It is reasonable to assume that those who generate and communicate information are motivated by a value framework which determines the kind of information they consider to be relevant. If this assumption is correct, and if information is an important determinant of wants, those who generate and communicate information have a key position in the decision making processes of society. While many have suspected this for a long time, its full implications for public decision making have not been fully explored. If the value frameworks of a relatively small number of individuals determine what information is generated and communicated, how might wants be altered if some other group of individuals with different value frameworks generated and communicated the information that helps determine wants? The implications of this question are of far-reaching importance to a society consisting of large organizations that tend to constrain individual actions and one which relies to such an extent upon mass media.

As is obvious from the foregoing comments, it is my judgment that the real "pay dirt" in a study of agenda setting lies in the stage of want formation and the translation of wants into demands. Certainly subsequent stages merit investigation and understanding, but my perceptions of the problem lead me to conclude that an examination of these early stages of the process will reveal more fundamental insights into the agenda-setting process than the later stages. Thus, instead of reducing the emphasis on the want-formation stage of the process, I would be inclined to give less emphasis to the later stages of agenda setting.

In offering these observations, I recognize the great difficulty of investigating in a rigorous way the issues I have emphasized. Possibly, in terms of the research program that RFF is sponsoring, a broad overview of the total process along the lines proposed by Davies is desirable as an initial effort. Possibly the investigation as outlined will provide a good basis for a deeper study of want formation to be undertaken later. In any event, I hope that such a study will not fail to get on the research agenda of RFF in the near future.

The Johns Hopkins University Press
This book was composed in Times Roman type by
Monotype Composition Company, Inc., from a
design by Susan Bishop. It was printed on
55-lb. Maple Danforth 350 paper and bound in
Joanna Arrestox cloth by The Maple Press
Company.

Library of Congress Cataloging in Publication Data

Main entry under title:

The Governance of common property resources.

  Includes bibliographies and index.
  1. Environmental policy—United States. I. Haefele,
Edwin T., ed. II. Resources for the Future.
HC110.E5G68   301.31'0973   74-6825
ISBN 0-8018-1650-5